P9-DVV-116

The Mom Friend

Guide to

→ EVERYDAY
SAFETY *and*
SECURITY

WITHDRAWN unty
COOPERATIVE LIBRARY SERVICES

The Mom Friend Guide to

EVERYDAY SAFETY and SECURITY

Tips from the Practical One in Your Squad

CATHY PEDRAYES

SIMON ELEMENT

New York   London   Toronto   Sydney   New Delhi

SIMON
ELEMENT

An Imprint of Simon & Schuster, Inc.
1230 Avenue of the Americas
New York, NY 10020

Copyright © 2022 by Cathy Pedrayes

All rights reserved, including the right to reproduce this book or portions thereof in any form whatsoever. For information, address Simon Element Subsidiary Rights Department, 1230 Avenue of the Americas, New York, NY 10020.

First Simon Element trade paperback edition April 2022

SIMON ELEMENT is a trademark of Simon & Schuster, Inc.

For information about special discounts for bulk purchases, please contact Simon & Schuster Special Sales at 1-866-506-1949 or business@simonandschuster.com.

The Simon & Schuster Speakers Bureau can bring authors to your live event. For more information or to book an event, contact the Simon & Schuster Speakers Bureau at 1-866-248-3049 or visit our website at www.simonspeakers.com.

Interior design by Jennifer Chung

Manufactured in the United States of America

1 3 5 7 9 10 8 6 4 2

Library of Congress Cataloging-in-Publication Data

Names: Pedrayes, Cathy, author. Title: The mom friend guide to everyday safety and security : tips from the practical one in your squad / by Cathy Pedrayes. Description: First Simon Element trade paperback edition. | New York, NY: Simon Element, 2022. Identifiers: LCCN 2021043104 (print) | LCCN 2021043105 (ebook) | ISBN 9781982185671 (paperback) | ISBN 9781982185688 (ebook) Subjects: LCSH: Preparedness. | Risk management. | Accidents—Prevention. | Data protection. Classification: LCC HV551.2 .P389 2022 (print) | LCC HV551.2 (ebook) | DDC 363.1—dc23
LC record available at https://lccn.loc.gov/2021043104
LC ebook record available at https://lccn.loc.gov/2021043105

ISBN 978-1-9821-8567-1
ISBN 978-1-9821-8568-8 (ebook)

33614082855031

Contents

The Mom Friend Guide to

EVERYDAY SAFETY and SECURITY

Introduction

I've been the Mom Friend of the group since my late teens. I didn't know the term for it then, but when I got my first car, I suddenly became responsible for others who rode with me, and I wanted to be prepared for anything that came our way.

Before I even drove my first car out of the driveway, my mom had equipped it with emergency lighting, blind spot mirrors, and a jump starter pack with an air compressor. To this day, I still carry most of those items in my car (upgraded, of course). As I got older and more experienced, I slowly added more and more to my list of safety must-haves.

I had always carried a basic first aid kit for cuts and blisters, but after an extensive first aid course, I took it to the next level and built a kit equipped to handle everything from a diabetic emergency to an extreme puncture. When I was the designated driver for drunk friends after a night at the club, my car was stocked with snacks, water, and baggies for nausea. When I drove my little sister around, she'd get carsick, so I always traveled with an extra change of clothes, paper towels, cleaning wipes, and bags for trash. But my preparedness didn't end with humans; I'm an animal lover, too, and growing up in Miami, I'd come across a lot of stray dogs and cats, so I began carrying leashes, food, bowls, and water for them in the trunk of my car. If there was a way I could help, I wanted to be prepared to do so.

These innate Mom Friend tendencies grew over time, which is precisely the genesis of this book. I've put my experiences into a reference guide so that you'll know where to start planning for safety and security, whether it's for your first car, first home, or a big trip. This book will cover some of the basics and some aspects that are not so basic, such as cybersecurity. Nearly everything comes from firsthand discussions or experiences, which I subsequently researched.

As I moved into adulthood, it seemed the greatest safety risks were on the road and at home, so that guided which supplies I stocked; but once I started working in television, I saw there was danger elsewhere. Starting out, I was twenty-six and a television host on a national network, which was reportedly viewed in more than one hundred million homes. My biggest concern was stalkers, and when I started working, I asked colleagues about their experiences; sure enough, nearly every person I spoke with had a scary story—in one case, the incident made national news. And how had these people found my coworkers? The internet. Stalking used to require being near someone to harass them or sending a letter in the mail, but with the internet and social media, anyone can do it from anywhere in the world. Which is how I learned about cybersecurity—out of a need to protect myself.

It may seem like an extreme scenario—not everyone works in television—but the truth is that when it comes to our digital lives, information is valuable. It doesn't take much for someone to run a search engine query with your name and find an address, emails, phone numbers, family members, and more. This information may not be used by a cyberstalker, but a hacker, identity thief, or anyone engineering a scam would love it. These are real threats millions of people experience every year, and much of it could be avoided with a little caution.

Of course, this is coming from the girl with millions of followers online, who still works in television, and who wrote a book—so don't think I'm the one who's going to tell you to hide in a compound somewhere. Nope! I've found that being prepared for scenarios (albeit some more likely than others) helps me react quickly when I come across them so I can avoid risky situations.

This book aims to make you aware of some of those situations, whether in the physical world or digital one, so that you're familiar with them and have some possible reactions and resources at the ready. But if a tip isn't for you, no worries. No one is going to quiz you at the end or judge you for not doing everything in these pages—you make the decisions that work best for you, and I hope this book will empower you to do so.

I'm excited to share this with you!

CHAPTER 1

MOM FRIEND AT HOME

O ur homes are our little oases. They're where we feel safe. They're where we make memories with our families and fur babies; they're where we relax and enjoy life. But they're also where we likely store most of our valuables. So despite the cozy feeling we get thinking about our home, it's also a source of risk. I won't get into all the data about the danger your home can harbor—ranging from home burglaries to injuries, fires, or assaults—but I will say that our homes are safest when we take a few steps to be prepared. Of course, nothing in this book is a fail-safe, but here's a quick guide to things that will help you feel (and be) more prepared at home.

Things That'll Help You Feel Safe, Inside and Out

Starting with the basics, here are a few items every home should have or avoid.

A carbon monoxide (CO) alarm: Carbon monoxide is a colorless, tasteless, odorless, and toxic gas that comes from anything that burns fuel, such as cars, fireplaces, gas stoves, water heaters, dryers, and more.

It's important we stay up-to-date on maintaining these items, but even so, equipment can malfunction. In order to keep our families safe, we need carbon monoxide alarms in our home (notice *alarms* is plural). Many experts recommend having one in every room so it can be heard, but in my home, I just have one on every floor. You can find them online and at hardware and big-box stores. If you have a security system, your service provider may sell some that are linked to emergency services. That said, make sure you have battery-operated ones as an additional precaution, or that there's a backup battery in case there's a power outage.

Smoke Alarms: You know the beep; we all know the beep. Sometimes they go off when the toaster smokes, but leave the batteries in because they're your earliest warning sign of a possible fire. It's best to have a smoke alarm in every sleeping room, in hallways, and on each floor of your home. It's also best to check them at least twice a year, and, if possible, you might want to opt for alarms that are monitored by the fire department. Your alarm system provider may offer this service (more on this later).

Fire extinguishers, blankets, and escape ladders: Most home fires start in a kitchen, so that's a great place to keep a fire extinguisher, but keep in mind that there are different types of fire extinguishers for different uses. Some are multipurpose, some are designed for electrical fires, some for regular household items, and some for grease fires. You may want a few different types in your home, and your local hardware store is a good place to find them. If you have a second story or accessible attic with a window, how about a window fire ladder? They're small, portable, and incredibly useful in the case of an emergency, and the same is true of fire blankets. They're a great way to smother a small fire caused by sources like cooking oil or fat. It's important to remember that when dealing with a grease fire, don't add water or flour; instead, smother it by covering it with a lid or baking sheet. Sand or baking soda are good for smothering a small grease fire (keyword "small"— unless you have a *ton* of baking soda or sand.)

Cameras: I'm a huge fan of cameras. I know that some of you may be concerned about Wi-Fi cameras being hacked, but my chapter on cyber threats will help you manage that risk, and in the worst-case scenario, you just unplug it. You can also take the precaution of not placing them in sensitive areas, like bedrooms. Instead, focus on placing them outside your home and add some indoors for when you're away and need to keep a closer eye on things.

As an alternative, you can use a camera that doesn't rely on Wi-Fi. These options are more limited and require professional installation, but they are harder to hack. That said, you may lose out on some of the benefits of a Wi-Fi camera, such as remote live footage, which is my favorite feature. Being able to see a live feed has a lot of benefits: it allows you to remotely monitor when loved ones get home, to see if an injury happens at your door in the moment, to be notified when packages are delivered, and, of course, to keep an eye on any suspicious activity.

But will you ever really need it? Almost definitely. Once, while on vacation, I was in a museum when I got an alert from my security system that a window had been broken at my home. I was several states away, but because of my cameras I was able to see that no one was inside. I also called police to check on my home and was able to see them and communicate with them via my exterior cameras to confirm that everything was okay. In this case, my cameras helped me have a sense of control rather than the panic I would've felt if I hadn't had my virtual eyes and ears.

So at minimum, I recommend a camera at your front door, like a doorbell camera, and if you can expand coverage, I advocate for coverage of every entrance to your home, including the back door and any side doors, mudroom doors, and basement doors.

If you're renting an apartment, your building may allow you to put a battery-powered camera at your front door, particularly if they don't already have surveillance in that area. The battery-powered cameras can be secured with a few screws, so they cause minimal damage, and since there's no hardwiring, they're easy to remove when you leave.

Home security system: A home security system can include an alarm, door sensors, window sensors, window-break sensors, motion sensors, temperature sensors, water-leak detectors, smoke detectors, and CO alarms. Ideally, you want a system that can communicate with emergency services directly if needed, and the newer systems also have smartphone apps, so you can remotely arm and disarm your home.

If you're renting, you may not be allowed to have a home security system professionally installed, but there are do-it-yourself options. You can also buy window entry sensors online and install them yourself. Installation usually requires only a sticker or small screws, so you don't need to be super handy.

Decoys: Whether you have an alarm or not, I recommend getting a security system sign or a Beware of Dog sign. The average home invader will think twice before targeting a dwelling with one of these signs. You can go as far as placing a large dog bowl in the yard or having one be visible from the window. No one wants to confront a scary dog, so having these decoys will not only scare away an amateur thief but can even send the pro burglar looking for an easier target.

You can try some other decoys as well. How about a toy police badge left on the kitchen counter? Or placing large, beat-up men's work boots at the door so it doesn't look like you live alone? Some security experts also suggest setting up burglar decoy smash-and-grab boxes. Because home invaders only spend about ten minutes inside, they probably don't have the time to really inspect their loot, so I suggest placing a box of seemingly valuable items in an obvious place like a nightstand drawer, sock drawer, or in your closet. In the box you can put some crumpled cash and fake jewelry. In an effort to quickly get away, a burglar might grab it and run, only to later realize it wasn't as valuable as they had hoped. It's better to distract a burglar with a decoy box than let them linger to find the good stuff.

Another way to set up some decoys is with smart-home devices. You can play the sound of people talking, a dog barking, trigger lighting, or you can have a little fun with it: There was a viral TikTok video of a family who set up their Amazon Alexa to respond to the command "Alexa, intruder." The Alexa immediately switched the lighting to dark red, started strobing it, and began a loud heavy metal song. In the presence of an intruder, I'd recommend running to safety over messing with Alexa, but if you can do it remotely, it's definitely scary and might just send the bad guys running—plus it's a good reminder to get creative!

Lighting: Believe it or not, lighting reduces crime, and it's actually been studied. Evidence from a randomized experiment of street lighting in New York City revealed that when communities were given more lighting, there was a 36 percent reduction in crime, specifically at night.[1]

The study may have been conducted in communities in New York City, but we can apply that same theory to our homes. I've never committed a crime, but if I had to put myself in the shoes of someone who did, I'd imagine the last thing someone would want is to get caught, and lighting increases the chances that you'd be seen, identified, and ultimately caught, so of course, a criminal avoids well-lit areas. This is why we're told not to walk down dark alleys alone. Well, that includes your house. Make sure there aren't any dark corners where someone can lurk. Pathways should be well lit, and you can opt for motion-sensing lights as well.

It's not only about criminal activity but overall safety. You're less likely to trip on a step if you can see it, and lighting will help you and anyone else be able to see those hazards and avoid getting hurt.

Landscaping: Similar to lighting, we don't want to create good hiding spots by letting our yards grow wild. In high-traffic areas, such as near your door, garage, and driveway, make sure you can see around you—a full 360 degrees—and if that means keeping the hedges short, it's worth it.

Landscaping can also be used as a deterrent. When I was growing up in Miami, my family constantly had people jumping the fences and walls into our yard. My mom came up with an easy solution—she planted cacti at the problem areas and it never happened again. Near my home, I've seen neighbors use these same tricks. They might plant thorny rosebushes, blackberries, acacia, firethorn, or agave near their front windows. You'll want to consider any fire-escape plans when planting, so where you place your spiky flora may vary based on the configuration of your home and general risk.

Locking doors and windows: This should be obvious, but I've found that not enough people regularly do this. Too often cars are stolen because doors are unlocked or windows are left open. It may seem simplistic, but locking a door really is a deterrent. I've seen it time and time again where a criminal simply walks away because the door is locked and moves on to an easier target. Of course, if someone wants to get in, they can always break a window to get into your home or car, but the random criminal is usually deterred by a simple lock. At home, check to make sure all of your windows and doors are locked, and if strangers have been inside (if you're having some construction done, for example), do a sweep after they leave to ensure all of the doors and windows are still locked. Also, if you have a door connecting your house to your garage, lock that door. Garages are easy to break into, even for the novice thief. That might be a problem if you have valuables in your garage, but it's also an issue if your garage door connects to your home. Simply locking that door might be enough of a deterrent should someone decide to take advantage of your vulnerable garage entryway. In addition, there are extra locks that you can get for your home in order to better protect yourself.

If you have a sliding glass door to your backyard or balcony, invest in a security bar. Sliding glass doors are pretty vulnerable, particularly older versions. They're generally easy to shimmy open or take off the track, and because they're made of glass, they can easily be broken. So for a few dollars, get a little extra security on your sliding glass doors.

Although you can put a wooden dowel along the track to keep the door from sliding open, there are more discreet ways to keep the door shut. You can install a door pin (this is probably the best option, but it takes a bit more skill) or a security bar. There are different alternatives, but adding even the simplest version is an inexpensive way to increase security.

Change your locks: When purchasing a new home, change your locks right away—you don't know how many people had the previous keys or who they were. When renting, ask your landlord to change your locks. If they give you a hard time, ask them whether they'll put in writing that they're taking on the liability should something happen to your home. That usually gets them to change their tune pretty quickly.

If your home has a garage code, the same advice applies. Set up a new code. As with the house keys, you don't know who had access to the previous code, or worse—maybe the code was never changed and it's an easy 0000 default. Case in point: in my neighborhood, there are a few well-known builders, so when my husband and I bought our home, the inspector told us he knew the security code simply because the builders tend to use the same one. Sure enough, he proceeded to open our garage door. Needless to say, changing our garage code was the first thing we did when we moved in.

Reinforce your door: This is an easy tip. Go to an exterior door of your home. Open it and unscrew the screws from the strike plate. Chances are they're half-inch screws, which make your door easier to kick down. All you need to do to make the door more secure is replace the screws in your door's strike plate with two-and-a-half- to four-inch screws, which are longer than average, thereby going into the framing of the house. This allows it to withstand more stress.

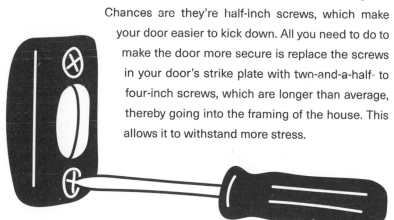

Personalized décor: Don't have personalized decals, doormats, mailboxes, or nameplates at your door. People can easily use them to obtain information about you.

This also presents a problem if you have a stalker. At the national television network I worked at, nearly every host had experienced some level of stalking. At least one case was severe, while others were simply obsessed fans who eventually went away; but one of the first things we were taught in safety training courses for the network was to stay away from personalized décor like doormats, because if someone was trying to check if they had the right home, that would easily give it away.

Kevlar gloves: This is totally optional, but after I got twenty-one stitches in my hand following a kitchen knife accident, I decided to invest in Kevlar gloves. When I'm cutting tough fruits or vegetables like watermelon, pumpkin, or squash, I get nervous with the tough skins, so I'll put my Kevlar gloves on before beginning. Kevlar gloves prevent a knife from cutting you with a slicing motion, but they're not puncture proof, so while they aren't a perfect solution, they help me feel more comfortable. They're also made of a soft fabric that you can wash, so you don't need to worry about cross contamination, but for extra protection you can put disposable gloves over the Kevlar gloves.

Flashlight: Where I grew up in Miami, we lost power frequently, and sometimes it was out for days. From that, I learned to always keep a flashlight by my bedside. Our phones have flashlights too, but in an emergency, you want to conserve power, so having flashlights and batteries are essential. You can also purchase windup flashlights, so you don't have to rely on batteries.

Window curtains: Use them; it's as simple as that. Especially at night. When it's dark out and the lights are on indoors while the curtains are open, there's a crystal clear view into your home. Your big-screen TV, computers, video game console—all of that is pretty easy to spot just by driving by for a few seconds. But if the curtains are closed, anyone would have to get a lot closer to your home to see those things, so at night, close your blinds. (During the day, I like to have them open because there are benefits to getting natural light into our homes for both our indoor health and mental health.)

Hiding spots: Several of my viral videos have focused on good hiding spots at home. If something is truly valuable, I'd recommend a safety-deposit box and/or a fireproof, waterproof safe that's bolted in your home, but for the other small things, here are a few ideas for where to hide them. What you want to remember is that not hiding things in obvious places is your best bet. A home intruder generally spends about ten minutes in a home, so they don't have time to look through every drawer and cabinet. Instead, they'll go for the obvious spots, like the primary bedroom, dresser drawers, closet, and office desks. But if you've hidden something at the bottom of your kitty litter, in a box of crackers in your kitchen pantry, or in a pile of clothes in the hamper, then chances are they won't have time to go through that. This doesn't only apply to home invasions—maybe you have a pet sitter you don't want to tempt or emergency cash you don't want the kids to find. Hiding spots are useful for a variety of reasons, and here are a few ideas:

- In the flour, sugar, cereal, crackers, or anything similar in your kitchen pantry

- Taped under a drawer

- Below the removable insole of a sneaker

- Inside a vacuum cleaner

- Under the bottom of a plant (outdoors, this is a common place to check for spare keys, so I don't recommend it there, but indoors it's a great hiding spot)

- In the basement or attic, hidden among home décor

- In your cleaning supplies area, and if you have some empty containers, you can clean them out and hide some things inside them

- In vents or false electrical outlets (in movies, these are common hiding spots, but if someone has limited time to get valuables and they don't know what they're looking for, it's unlikely they're going to go room to room with a screwdriver checking your vents or looking for a false electrical outlet)

- In the laundry detergent or with clothes in a hamper

- In the pet food or kitty litter pan

- Beneath the cover of an ironing board

- In the refrigerator or freezer in a container with food like frozen veggies

- Inside the spring rod of a toilet paper holder

- In an empty spice jar hidden with your spices

- Among your feminine products or baby diapers

- In an empty deodorant container or lip balm

- In an old paint can

- In a slit-open tennis ball hidden among the pets' or kids' toys

- In diversion safes; there are plenty of options, from fake books to fake plumbing pipes, that are large enough to hold some cash, jewelry, and other small valuables or important documents

Neighbors: Get to know your neighbors. You don't have to be besties, but friendly neighbors can keep an eye on your property when you're not around or let you know when an unusual "technician" was seen roaming around the property, and in case of an emergency, you'll know where to go for help.

Keep a binder listing your valuables: If there's a thief, a storm, or some other disaster, keeping good records will make things easier for you when dealing with insurance companies and police. When you purchase valuables such as jewelry, electronics, tools, or home appliances, keep your receipts, record serial numbers, and photograph your items. In the case of theft, police can use this information to scout local pawn shops. If you're dealing with insurance companies or manufacturer warranties, they'll need this information as well, so keep good records. In case of crisis, it's also helpful to have quick access to passports, birth certificates, copies of social security cards, your marriage license, contact information for insurance brokers, financial managers, etc. You can keep this information digitally, but it's worth having a hard copy hidden in your home in case of an emergency.

Maintenance: Maintaining your home is also part of keeping it safe. If the first-floor window lock is having trouble locking or your garage never closes right, then get it fixed. Don't leave tools or ladders lying around the yard. They may be valuable enough to steal on their own or be used to gain entry into your home. If you do keep tools outdoors, get a lockable shed for storage.

Also, when installing things like window AC units, make sure they're installed properly so you're not inadvertently giving away an easy access point to your home. The same is true of holiday decorations; to hang things like Christmas lights, sometimes people will run lines through their windows, thereby leaving the window unlocked, which might just invite an unwanted houseguest.

Ultimately, thieves look for easy marks, so maintaining your home makes you less likely to be targeted.

Location: When you're looking to move into a new home, it's important to consider your location. What's around the prospective home? Is the apartment on a ground floor? If so, is it accessible by foot? Are there bars on the windows or any preventative measures in place to deter break-ins? Will you be taking public transit from this new home? If so, what does the route look like? Is it well-lit and populated?

Think about what your new routine will look like from this new home and make sure that you're comfortable with it before committing to a lease or a mortgage. Also, do a quick search about crime in the area and to get a feel for the neighborhood. There are sites that maintain neighborhood statistics, such as neighborhoodscout.com, crimegrade. org, and areavibes.com, but you can also use community groups. You can check Facebook groups, nextdoor.com, or apps like Citizen or Ring, where users share videos and report crimes. These resources, particularly the apps, may not be available to everyone or applicable in every city, but it's worth knowing they exist for those who are able to take advantage of them. Also, once you are living in your new neighborhood, these community groups are a great way to stay on top of what's happening locally, whether or not it's related to crime.

Get a dog: If you've ever wanted a dog, great news! You can officially use your personal safety as an excuse, because they're a great alarm system. Not only can they alert you to a problem but they can be a deterrent as well. Of course, only commit to a dog if you're prepared for a lifelong commitment and have the time and financial resources, but if you were looking for a reason to take the leap, you have it now! As an alternative to a long-term commitment, try fostering dogs.

I've worked with animal rescues since I was in college but have unofficially been rescuing animals since I was a child. Many animal rescues will cover the expenses of fostering a dog, which serves as a good test run if you're unsure of the commitment while allowing you to get the benefits of a little extra security. (Full disclosure: When you first get a foster dog, expect accidents. Even fully potty-trained dogs are bound to have accidents until they acclimate to your schedule. A rescue organization can walk you through the expectations, but as someone who's fostered tons of pets and has their own, I highly recommend it.)

Your trash: When getting rid of paper mail, always shred the important documents like credit card offers, medical documents, or utility bills. Also look at packages that are mailed to your home—oftentimes the label includes your name, address, and phone number. Personally, I like to remove the stickers and shred them, but when I'm feeling lazy and the mail isn't that personal, I use an identity-theft protection stamp. It covers confidential information with randomized letters, and most of these stamps work on glossy paper (test this out at home by smudging the paper and wetting it to see if the ink runs). Blotting it out with a black marker doesn't work, because if you simply tilt the paper toward the light, you can see right through the marker. An identity-theft protection stamp is much more efficient, and you can even use it on things that are difficult to shred, like medicine bottles.

Also important is to actually take your trash in and out. A clear sign that someone isn't home is a trash bin that's been sitting out by the curb for too long or a house that didn't put out a bin at all when the rest of the neighborhood has. That might just mean the house is sitting empty. And along those same lines, when you purchase a big-ticket item like a new computer or game console, consider dumping the box on your own instead of leaving it by the driveway. Leaving the box in plain sight lets everyone know you just got a new shiny, expensive toy. Another option is to break down the box and place it in the recycling bin or turn it inside out, so the logos aren't showing, and then cover it with other regular boxes. You can also keep it inside until you see the recycling or garbage truck passing by and then run it out, so it's not sitting out overnight like a giant billboard.

Your mail: When I was younger, I was taught not to use my full name when putting my return address on envelopes. The theory was that someone could identify me as a woman and act in a discriminatory fashion. Ever since, I've always used a first initial with my last name. When I first posted this tip online, I found that many other women did the same thing. The truth is, we don't know where our mail ends up when it gets sent out. Is it shredded? Tossed in the trash? Recycled? Where does that go? Our trash may not even stay within the country, so to minimize how many times my name is floating around out there, I shred any incoming mail and outgoing mail gets initials. Now with so much information online, this tip may be outdated, but we all still send and receive mail, so it is something to keep in mind.

Another thing I do with my mail is I change my name when I ship items to myself. For example, if I order a package from Amazon, it gets delivered to "Cathy Amazon." If I order something from Target, the package will say "Cathy Target." I could address the package to "Cathy's Shopping Emporium" if I wanted to—the courier delivers based off the address. Why do I do this? For cybersecurity purposes. If my information were to get sold or stolen from a company I ordered from, I should be able to track the leak with my fake last name.

Once data companies or hackers purchase lists of names, they rarely clean up their lists. They simply use a software to automate the task they'd like to perform and let it go from there—which means my name on these lists would show up as Cathy Amazon or Cathy Target and I would easily be able to track the leak or data sold to the business responsible. What I would eventually do with the information would depend on the companies' privacy policies.

In my experience in the United States, doing that has never affected the delivery of my mail, but if you're concerned that it may be a problem, you can use your full name but add a code. For example, I could be "Cathy AMZ Pedrayes," and I would know the package is something I ordered from Amazon.

Delivery safes: Package thefts are a common occurrence, and depending on where you live, you may be able to invest in a simple deterrent: a delivery safe. They come in a variety of sizes, and some are even insulated for grocery deliveries. They generally have a keypad with a code you can give to delivery personnel, and you can change this code as often as you'd like. There's usually an administrative code as well as a key for backup. In order for delivery safes to work at preventing theft, they do need to be bolted to the ground, so if you're renting, you'll likely need permission to install a delivery safe.

Home safe: For high-value items that you don't need quick access to, I'd recommend a safety-deposit box, but if you want quick access, then get a home safe and make sure it's bolted into the floor or ceiling. Home safes are an absolute must for firearms, particularly when there are children in the home or in the case of theft. Where I grew up in Miami, water damage is always top of mind, given the hurricanes, floods, and infrastructure breaking down. Instead of risking your most valuable items getting waterlogged, get a safe that's waterproof and built with fire-resistant materials. Some important items to keep in a safe could include insurance documents, financial documents, cash, jewelry or other collectibles, family photos, safety-deposit keys (if you have one), a home inventory list or your emergency binder, and external computer hard drives. And if you want a safe with all the top-notch features, try going directly to a manufacturer that specializes in safes. They'll be able to help you pick the right one.

Smart-home devices: Some feel smart-home devices like Amazon Alexa or Google are invasive and untrustworthy, while others feel the benefits outweigh the risks. At the moment, I'm in the latter category. Should anything go wrong, I can easily unplug a device, but I like having the added control. If I'm away from home, I can use my smart lighting or smart plugs to make it look like I'm home. Cameras help me keep an eye on things, and devices like the Alexa can act as extra security, listening for glass breaking or even calling the police if needed (it's a paid feature). The downside is that if there's a power outage, you lose all the benefits, but that's true of any electronic device.

Nonlethal protection: You're probably familiar with some of the traditional home protection measures involving weapons, but sometimes the thought of having a lethal weapon in our homes is concerning.

It could be because we have young children in the home, because we don't have the time to receive proper training, or maybe it's simply difficult to obtain—in any case, there are nonlethal alternatives to protecting our homes. My preferred nonlethal tool is a pepper spray gun. It's kind of like a paintball gun. The rounds are filled with nonlethal powdered pepper spray and tear gas that break upon contact. It causes temporary blindness and difficulty breathing, so it's effective while still being safe. The main reason why I prefer a pepper spray gun over the traditional versions is that a pepper spray gun is effective from more than one hundred feet away (similar to a handgun), while traditional pepper spray is effective six to ten feet from your target. Preferably, we want to be as far away from a dangerous situation as possible, so the more distance, the better. Pepper spray guns are also generally powered by CO_2 (you typically buy this separately), which means when the pellet shoots out of the gun, it's going to have some impact when it hits someone—so you'll inflict some cuts or bruises while still using a nonlethal form of force. And while it's certainly safer to have in homes with children, that doesn't mean it should be left unattended as a toy. Keep it locked up, away from children.

Please note that as with traditional pepper spray devices, restrictions on pepper spray vary by state, so you'll have to check your local regulations. If you go to a website to purchase pepper spray and your area isn't listed as an available shipping region, it's probably because there's a local regulation blocking pepper spray sales there.

Social media: I discuss this in depth in the cybersecurity chapter and touch on it again in the vacation chapter, but for now let me remind you that social media is part of your home's safety. Before posting photos with an address in the background, showing where you keep your valuables, or admitting that you're away from home on vacation, consider the risk. I know the vacation one is tough, but risk is different for every person. Where is your house located? Do you have cameras? Neighbors you can call or family nearby? A pet or house sitter coming by to check in regularly? Smart lighting to make it look like someone is home? Are you renting in a building with hundreds of apartments? Is there a door-man providing security? If I'm considering how risky a post is, these aspects help me feel more comfortable, but of course, every person's home and situation is different. That said, my official recommendation is to not post about your vacation while you're away.

Privacy film: My front door used to have decorative windows that allowed anyone who stood at the door to look into my home—from a delivery person to a solicitor I was trying to avoid, or a friendly neighbor—but I was uncomfortable with this, so I installed privacy film. There are a variety of films available; some look like decorative mosaic glass, others mimic a one-way mirror, and then there's some blackout film that will completely block anyone from looking into the window. With most privacy film, it's important to note that it works well during the day, but at night if the lights are on, it's ineffective. Even during the day, someone could theoretically get up close and peak in or even use their phone camera to do it. So if you want full privacy, go with blackout film. The downside for that option is that you won't be able to look out, so you'll need another method to see who's at the door, like a peephole, a door camera, or another window nearby.

Your keys: A common question that I get is where to hide your spare key. The short answer is don't. If you need to have access to a spare key directly outside your home, this is where you can rely on a trust-worthy neighbor or family. Keys hidden under doormats, rocks, and potted plants or above the doorframe are too easy to find. And why risk it? Either give a spare to someone you trust or invest in a smart lock. With a smart lock, you don't have to worry about hiding a key outside your home, because it's keyless entry. Instead of fumbling with keys, you can program a smart lock to recognize when you're at the door or use a code to unlock it. The downside is, again, that a power outage can leave you locked out if you don't have a backup key, and as with any technology, no matter how secure it is, it can still be tampered with.

Your smartphone: If you're using any home security devices on your smartphone, make sure that your phone is locked with a code in case it's lost or stolen. Also know that you can wipe your phone remotely. Whether it's an Apple or an Android, you can log into your Google account or your iCloud and remotely wipe your phone or lock it with lost mode. Additionally, you should set up your phone to automatically back up every day, so if it's lost or stolen, you won't lose all your data.

Childproofing: If you have children or curious pets, childproofing electrical outlets, sharp corners, and cabinets containing cleaning supplies or medications is essential, but childproofing kits can also provide extra home security. For example, door lever locks are typically used to keep kids from opening doors, but if you're in an apartment, you can also use them to keep landlords out when they don't have permission to enter, or as backup security measures. If you have sliding doors, child-safety door locks can also help reinforce those. It may not be a perfect or high-tech security system, but any deterrent, no matter how small, is still a deterrent and you never know what you prevented if you prevented it.

Hidden dangers: When we think of dangers in the home, the first thing that comes to mind are likely kitchen accidents or potential fires, but there are other hidden dangers within our home, particularly when it comes to our furry family members. You probably already keep the more obvious dangers locked away, like medications and chemicals, but there are many common household items that are poisonous to cats and dogs. Here are a few common ones:

- **Houseplants:** Before bringing plants into the house, make sure they won't harm your cat or dog. For example, Easter lilies can cause severe kidney failure in cats. Poinsettias are also mildly toxic to dogs and cats. Other common plants that our furry friends shouldn't consume include aloe vera, tomato plants, amaryllises, gladiolas, daffodils, tulips, and so many more. All of these can cause a variety of health issues for pets, including serious illness or even death. If you have a curious pet who's known to munch on plants in the house or garden, make sure you're not bringing anything into your home that is poisonous and supervise your pets.

- **Flea and tick shampoos:** Before using a flea and tick shampoo on your pet, read the directions to ensure it's appropriate. Often, a shampoo that's meant for dogs cannot be used on cats or even near a cat. Also, many shampoos cannot be used on puppies that are under a certain weight or under ten to twelve weeks of age, but every product is different, so it's important to read the directions before we use these items on our pets. If you're not sure, you can call your vet and look for alternatives online.

- **Using human products on pets:** When it comes to bathing and caring for our pets, only use items that have been specifically formulated for your pet or approved by your veterinarian. Even using something as simple as human shampoo on a cat can have damaging effects.

- **Minoxidil:** Minoxidil is a topical solution that's used to promote hair growth in humans, but it's been found to be highly toxic for cats, which means if you're using a hair-growth stimulant like Rogaine, you should keep it far away from your cat. Your feline shouldn't bite your hair, lick your pillowcase, or even walk through a spill of the product. It's more toxic to cats than dogs, but that doesn't mean dogs aren't affected. Be on the safe side and steer clear of using it around your pets.

- **Xylitol:** This is an artificial sweetener found in a lot of products that are labeled as sugar-free, like chewing gum, peanut butter, syrup, and even toothpaste. It's extremely toxic to dogs. Be careful before sharing food with your pets, and when you're stuffing their toys with peanut butter or brushing their teeth, make sure the ingredients don't include xylitol, or you may inadvertently be poisoning your pet.

- **Food:** Some favorite human foods like chocolate, grapes, raisins, garlic, onions, leeks, chives, macadamia nuts, coffee, and more can be toxic for pets. Even some of their favorites like cheese and dairy can be harmful to cats and dogs in excessive quantities. It's okay to share some foods with your pets, but make sure it's something simple. Ingredients you've seen advertised on pet food bags are a good gauge, for example: grilled chicken (no bones or spices), rice, sweet potato, pumpkin, peas, carrots, blueberries, and salmon are all foods our dogs and cats can ingest, but it's also important to ask your vet. Some pets may have allergies or other issues that make foods that are generally safe unsuitable for them, so always check first.

Twenty-four-hour poison control hotlines exist for both humans and pets. The human hotline is free while the pet hotline charges a nominal fee. Luckily, I haven't had to use the human poison control hotline, but once during my college years, I had to use it for my dog, who had gotten into a bunch of chocolate. It was the middle of the night and I lived in a remote area, so I called the poison control hotline for help. They answered quickly and told me to induce vomiting using hydrogen peroxide. You already know that as a Mom Friend, I was equipped with my stocked first aid kit that had hydrogen peroxide and a syringe. Crisis successfully resolved.

I highly recommend having your home equipped with all the basics to address first aid for both pet and human needs, plus having the poison control hotline phone numbers at the ready. Maybe tape them to the side of the refrigerator or on the garage door; either way, be sure to put them in a place where you can quickly access them in case of an emergency. For more information and resources, check with your local vet.

Fire safety: According to the 2020 National Fire Protection Association report "Fire Loss in the United States during 2019,"[2] a home fire is reported every ninety-three seconds in the US, and aside from some of the tools I mentioned, there are habits that can help protect us. Did you know sleeping with your door closed can help save your life or a loved one's life in the case of a fire? It's remarkable to think your average wooden bedroom door can have such an effect, but it's true. If the doors in your home are closed, it helps slow the spread of a fire, keeps the temperature down in the rooms, and keeps carbon monoxide levels down. The Fire Safety Research Institute (FSRI) has a campaign called "Close Before You Doze" to educate people about this, and they've done demos showing how much of an impact a closed door has. It's so simple but so important.

That tip was one of my first viral videos, and the comments were filled with people who couldn't believe it was true, people who said their pets wouldn't let them (#catmom!), and people who said they learned firsthand how important closing your door is. The truth is that a home fire today is more dangerous than it was forty years ago. Modern homes have open floor plans, synthetic construction materials, and flammable furniture, all of which burn rather quickly. The FSRI reports that forty years ago, people had seventeen minutes to escape a home fire, but today it's an average of three minutes.[3] And feel free to close more doors than just the bedroom, as the less air the fire gets, the more time you and your family have to get out. I think back to my overprotective family who never let me close the door—if only I had been equipped with this fire safety information as a teen! If your children sleep in a separate room, closing the door can protect them in the case of a fire. If there's smoke, you may not have time to run to them, but with their door closed, you'll know they'll have more time to survive that situation. It's a scary thought, but what I find scarier is that this simple hack isn't more well-known.

If, for whatever reason, it's not practical to close bedroom doors in your home, smoke alarms are key. They provide your earliest warning signs of a possible fire, and if you can't get out of the house when you hear a smoke alarm going off, run to a room with a window located as far away from the fire as possible. Close the door, call emergency services, stay low to the floor, and cover vents and cracks under doors with clothing, towels, and whatever else is available. If smoke is getting into the room, open the window to keep the smoke above your head and stay near it so you can get fresh air. You can also signal where you are by waving a shirt, your hand, or a flashlight out the window or calling out for help. Remember: Plan A is always to escape through the closest door or window, but if you can't do that, go to plan B. And don't forget to call emergency services! Every house is different, so come up with the best escape routes for your home.

Here's a list of other habits we should get into to protect ourselves from fires at home:

- **Heaters:** If you're using a space heater, make sure there's nothing around it that can catch fire, like clothing or bedding, and shop for a heater that has safety features like an auto shutoff if it's knocked over. Also, if you have pets or children, try to shop for a heater that stays cool to the touch.

- **Dryer lint:** Every time you use a dryer, clean the lint screen. Dryer fires are pretty common in the US and the primary cause is a buildup of lint. Cleaning out the screen not only helps prevent that but also helps your machine run more efficiently. Also, if you can avoid running the dryer when you're not home to watch it, that's recommended.

- **Dust:** Similar to lint, dust is flammable, and when it builds up on vents, electrical sockets, or near electronics, it's a hazard since these are all sources of heat. As if allergies weren't enough of a reason, here's one more reason to dust and clean.

- **Toaster:** When you toast bread, it's likely that crumbs are left behind, and over time these crumbs can build up, meaning the next time you try to make toast, you might end up with a fire that toasts your kitchen. There's an easy fix: clean out the crumb tray and/or shake your toaster upside down over the trash to remove the crumbs (I like to do both).

- **Range hood:** If you have a vent over your stove and you cook a lot, make sure you clean the vent every month or so. When we're cooking, grease can build up in our vents and present a fire hazard. Even if you order a ton of takeout, dust can build up in the range hood, so it's still worth cleaning every few months.

- **Batteries:** Storing batteries properly, particularly nine-volt batteries, can help prevent a fire. Nine-volt batteries are dangerous because the positive and negative posts are close together. So if we throw them in our junk drawer, they can come in contact with something metal in the drawer, like a loose screw, and start a fire. An easy fix is to keep the batteries in their packaging or cover the posts with electrical tape. The same applies when we throw them out—put electrical tape on the posts before tossing them into the trash.

- **Light bulbs:** I've definitely had those lazy moments when I pop a bulb into a lamp without even thinking about the wattage—if the thing turns on, it must be fine. That is a deadly misconception. Incorrect wattage can be dangerous and lead to an electrical fire. It's important not to overload our lamps and lighting by putting bulbs in with wattage that's too high for the unit.

- **Extension cords:** If we overload extension cords by connecting a bunch of them, they can short-circuit and cause a fire, so don't abuse them—and also don't cover them. I know cables and cords can be unsightly, but if we hide them under a rug, they can overheat the rug (which is likely made of synthetic material), and that's a recipe for disaster. Let the cords breathe, and if you need more outlets, hire an electrician.

- **The stove:** Most home fires start in the kitchen, and the stove is the biggest offender. A grease fire is the most common kitchen fire, which can quickly get out of control, and usually it's because someone left the stove unattended as they were cooking. That's a big no-no. If you have to step away, turn off the heat.

- **Candles:** They're sublime. We love them, but unless they're flameless, don't leave them unattended, and keep them away from anything flammable. Also, don't let them get dusty, since dust is flammable. And if a flame ever gets too high for comfort, remember to smother it.

Things That Will Help You Feel Prepared: First Aid

My knowledge of first aid is how I earned my reputation as the Mom Friend of my squad. In one of my first viral TikTok videos, I shared some less-common items that I keep in my first aid kit. Within minutes, the comments were full of people calling me the "Mom Friend of the group," a badge I now wear with pride, but it wasn't always that way.

Learning first aid tips wasn't even a thought until my little sister was born. I was home for the summer from college, she was two years old, and as I was bathing her, I noticed she'd squirm when water would go near her ear. I didn't think much of it, but as I was telling my mom about how strange she was with water, my mom immediately identified an ear infection. This scared me.

I knew the ear infection would be treated, but I was scared because I now didn't trust myself to babysit. I didn't recognize the signs of an ear infection, I didn't notice her squirming as a sign of discomfort or pain, and I realized that if there was an injury, I wouldn't know what to do.

The guilt I felt in that moment made me commit to learning first aid. I knew that in order to feel confident taking care of my little sister, I needed to know what to do in emergency situations and how to identify risks. I quickly signed up for a semester-long first aid course, which proved to be much more in-depth than a traditional course. What I learned there I later shared on TikTok.

I don't know why that video or any of my subsequent videos went viral. It's a mystery of the algorithm, but I suspect it's because many of us, no matter our age, have likely witnessed an accident or injury and didn't feel prepared to react. We call for help, but help can take time, so what happens while you wait? Do you panic, or do you act?

I recommend taking a first aid course—it's the best way to learn how to use what you'll find in many first aid kits, and it will help you act quickly. But as with most things, technology can help guide us along as well. The American Red Cross has first aid apps for humans and pets with language functionality that switches between English and Spanish. It can help you identify the emergency; you can take quizzes to help you gauge what you've learned, and you can even locate hospitals or call emergency services directly from the app. I still recommend a course, but the app is a great way to stay up-to-date or read up on information before or after a first aid course.

In the meantime, here are a few first aid kit items that will quickly earn you the reputation of being the Mom Friend of the group.

HOW DO I PREPARE A FIRST AID KIT?

First aid kits will vary based on the scenario. What you keep in your purse will be different from what you keep at work or at home, but let's start with an at-home kit.

Most accidents happen at home, and of those accidents, most happen in the kitchen and bathroom, so having a first aid kit near those rooms is a good first step.

What do we put in our kits?

- **A list of nearby clinics, hospitals, their hours of operation, and emergency phone numbers.**

    This is essential. If an accident happens at home, do you know where the closest emergency facility is to you? Are they open twenty-four hours? Make a list of these facilities and keep their information updated and accessible. Don't forget to include places for your pets as well.

    You may think you can look these up on your phone if needed, which is true, but it'll save you time to have a list ready versus looking up nearby clinics, hours, and locations in your time of need.

- **Latex, nitrile, or vinyl gloves in various sizes.**

    If there's exposure to blood or bodily fluids, you need gloves. Also keep in mind that some people have latex allergies, so you may want to have a few glove options in your kit.

- **Sterile gauze pads and roller gauze.**

    The pads are great for small wounds or burns, while the roller gauze can be used for larger areas.

- **Adhesive bandages (different sizes).**
  These are generally for cuts and scrapes, but bandages can also be combined with sterile gauze or dressings to help hold them in place.

- **Trauma dressings and/or sanitary napkins (pads).**
  Pads aren't sterile, but they're a good backup if you don't have sterile trauma dressings. Both are meant for larger wounds when you need something more absorbent.

- **Bandages.**
  Bandages are meant to hold a dressing in place, and they can apply pressure to control bleeding, reduce swelling, and provide support. There are techniques on how to apply them and which ones to use for different situations (this is where that first aid course comes in), but for an at-home kit, I'd recommend the roller gauze and the elastic bandages as a starter.

- **Disposable instant cold packs.**
  At home you may have some frozen peas in the freezer, but it's always good to have instant cold packs on hand as an alternative.

- **Plastic bags.**
  I like to keep zippered bags in my kit in case I need to use them as an ice pack, to keep a wound dry, or for transporting things that need to be kept clean and dry.

- **Scissors.**
  These are useful for cutting gauze or cutting away clothing from a wound.

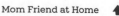

- **Tweezers.**
    Tweezers can be used to remove bee stingers, splinters, or pieces of glass in cuts, among other things.

- **Rubbing alcohol or hydrogen peroxide.**
    Contrary to popular belief, rubbing alcohol and hydrogen peroxide shouldn't be used on open wounds. They can cause tissue damage and slow healing (this was probably one of the most shocking things I learned in my first aid courses, because I'd been using both on cuts for years). The best way to clean wounds is with mild soap and water. Alcohol is for cleaning your tools, such as tweezers, while hydrogen peroxide is great for general cleaning and is used in certain pet emergencies, so I always have both on hand.

- **Safety pins.**
    Safety pins can pin back clothes or secure bandages—they're just good to have.

- **Antibiotic ointment.**
    This can be used to prevent bacterial infections in small cuts, burns, and scrapes.

- **Antiseptic skin wipes.**
    These wipes are a gentle way to cleanse an area when soap and water aren't available.

- **Calamine lotion.**
    Use calamine lotion to treat poison oak, poison ivy, insect bites, minor burns, rashes, etc.

- **Hydrocortisone cream.**
    Hydrocortisone cream reduces itching, swelling, and redness, and can be used for many of the same things we

use calamine lotion for—minor rashes, insect bites, and other reactions, such as allergies.

- **Over-the-counter medications.**
  Consult with your doctor, but have something on hand for pain, fever, allergies, an upset stomach, and cold and cough. Eye drops are helpful as well. Feel free to add to the list and personalize for your home.

- **Optional: CPR rescue mask.**
  If you've taken a CPR course and know the technique, it's worth adding a CPR rescue mask to your kit and including sizes for adults and children.

- **Optional: Choking Rescue Mask**
  This is a backup device for use when traditional first aid methods aren't successful. It's basically a plunger attached to a face mask that creates suction to remove an airway obstruction. It's easy to use— you can even use it on yourself—and manufacturers offer masks for adults and children. The most popular brands I've come across are LifeVac and Dechoker.

And remember to stay on top of expiration dates!

CHAPTER 2

PERSONAL SAFETY: THINGS TO CARRY WITH YOU

In a perfect world, this chapter wouldn't have to exist. We should feel safe at all times, never having to question whether someone's lurking behind a corner. Most of the time we probably do feel safe (that's a good thing—it means your gut is working), but other times we catch a creepy vibe that makes the hairs on the back of our neck stand up. The information that I provide here is to address things we can carry with us to help us in dangerous situations or, better yet, avoid them altogether.

Zap and spray: When you think of a self-defense tool you can carry with you, a taser, stun gun, or pepper spray probably come to mind first. I personally prefer tools that give me some range, like pepper spray or a taser, but all have their downsides. The biggest problem is that their legal restrictions vary, and they're probably not appropriate for all ages. This is the main reason why I don't talk about them much on my social media pages, but I mention them here because it's worth noting that in places where they're permitted, they're small enough to tuck into a purse and carry with you. Keep in mind that there's a difference between a stun gun and a taser. A stun gun is more of a visual deterrent, while a taser has probes that become embedded in a person's body.

Smart jewelry or SOS device: Wearable safety devices like smart jewelry are one of my favorite safety items. For one, they don't look like protection—they blend in with whatever you're wearing, and they are available in a bunch of different styles. What I find to be most beneficial about these devices is that a button is hidden in a bracelet or a necklace. If you push the button twice, the device can send an SOS call or text to your emergency contacts and police with your location. Safety jewelry or SOS devices are available from a variety of retailers, but some of my favorite brands include invisaWear, Flare, and Silent Beacon. These tend to have higher retail prices, but they don't have monthly app subscription fees (unless you want to upgrade), and I prefer their designs.

The reason why I'm partial to a wearable device like smart jewelry is that in the case of an emergency where I'm running from someone or trying to call for help without bringing attention to myself, I probably won't have time to grab anything in my purse, and even if my phone is in my pocket, it's tough to run while you're reaching for your back pocket. In my theoretical emergency situations, a bracelet or scrunchie or necklace with a safety button is a lot easier to access in a pinch.

The only downside is that because they're generally Bluetooth devices, you do need to be within range of your phone. In my theoretical situations, my phone is always on me but not accessible, so I don't see that as a major drawback.

Smartphones and apps: Speaking of items that are always on us, let's talk about our phones for a second. Our phones have a variety of safety features built in, and if not, there's usually an app that'll pick up the slack. Location sharing is included in every smartphone. It's not to be abused, but when your spouse is late getting home from work, your friend is going on a first date, or your daughter is going on her first interview, location sharing gives you some comfort in knowing where your loved one is.

Within your phone you can also set up emergency contacts and medical information. When you use the SOS feature, the phone sends a message with your location to your emergency contacts and emergency personnel. You can also have it share your medical information, which is particularly important if you have any allergies (this is something you have to set up ahead of time and keep up-to-date). It will allow first responders to access the information in an emergency, and you can set it up to automatically transmit the information during an emergency call (on an iPhone it's called Medical ID; you can find it in the Health app). Check your specific phone model for exactly how to use the SOS feature, but usually it involves clicking a button on the phone five times quickly.

Those are built-in features that come with your phone, but there are other apps with safety features too. Some messaging apps also have a location-sharing feature. WhatsApp is a messaging app that allows you to share your location with a designated emergency contact, and you can even set up a timer so the location sharing expires automatically, or you can turn it off manually.

You can also create shortcuts on your phone. One of the most well-known safety shortcuts on the iPhone is called "Siri, I'm Getting Pulled Over." You can copy most of the Apple shortcuts with Google Assistant, but essentially, if you get pulled over and trigger the shortcut, it will set off twenty-five actions, including location sharing and video recording that's sent to your emergency contacts and uploaded to the cloud.

Those features are free, but there are also paid apps that you can download for a one-time fee or a monthly subscription. Some apps are free as well but have a fee for full functionality. If you want the ability to call someone 24-7 for those moments when you're getting out of work late or need an emergency "get me outta here" call, then there are apps that can do that. You can even schedule an app to time out an activity, and if you don't turn off the timer, it'll automatically call emergency services.

Functionality may vary a bit, and there are always new apps in development, but some popular safety apps include Noonlight, Life360 (for location sharing), Citizen, Sekura, bSafe, and SoSecure. Wearable safety devices also have their own apps.

Transportation apps: Chances are you've used a ridesharing app service like Uber or Lyft, particularly if you live in or have traveled to a city. For both the drivers and the passengers, safety is a concern, but from a rider perspective, many of these apps include a ton of safety features. When you're traveling, whether it's local or abroad, get familiar with the transportation app you're using before taking a ride.

For example, Uber, arguably the most notable ridesharing service, has several in-app safety features. You can share your trip with trusted contacts and even set up reminders so that you don't forget to share your trip details. You can call or text your driver with an in-app anonymous number so you don't have to give away personal information; plus, the app also has a driver profile where you can see their photo, rating, license plate, how long they've been driving, and more, so you can feel confident you're getting into the right car. Another way to do this is to set up the PIN-verification feature where your driver will have to verify a PIN in order to confirm they're your driver; you can utilize that feature every trip you take or only for evening trips. You can also set up RideCheck in the app, which tracks your route. If it goes off course or if you're stopped for a long time, the app will send you a notification requesting confirmation that everything is okay. It can even detect if there's been a crash, and if the app detects something has gone wrong, it will send you a notification to check on you. If there's an issue, you can report it within the app, which includes calling an emergency number or the Critical Safety Response Line, sharing a trip with a friend, reporting a crash, and more. Remember that the features can vary based on the country you're in, but each app has its own set of features. Lyft offers a lot of what Uber does, just with different names.

In most cases, you'll feel perfectly comfortable using a rideshare service, but even so, it's nice to know the apps have built-in features to help you feel even more comfortable. And if you have a Mom Friend who wants to make sure you're getting home safe, you can always easily share your trip details. So, when you're downloading a rideshare app (or any app), take some time to get familiar with the options in the settings, whether it's safety features, securing your account, or making sure the app isn't selling your data. Get into the habit of familiarizing yourself with the app so you know what it does.

Hidden safes: Whether you're traveling abroad or through the city to get to work, hidden safes might just do the trick to keep your valuables out of sight. Instead of carrying all of your cash in a purse, how about mixing it up by putting some in a water bottle that has a hidden screw-on safe at the bottom? Or a scarf with a hidden zipper pocket? Often people use these hidden safes for a little extra privacy, as well as to hide more discreet items, like feminine products. I've heard from teenagers who use scrunchies with a hidden zipper pocket for their feminine products, so when they're at school, they don't have to try to hide them in the palms of their hands. Not that there's any shame in going to the restroom or carrying feminine products, but sometimes we prefer a little extra privacy, and that's okay. Some people also use them to hide snacks in theaters, and they're great when visiting concert halls that don't let you bring purses or backpacks, in which case, a scarf with a hidden zipper pocket is perfect to carry your wallet, phone, and keys.

Your keys: Many of us have thought about using our keys as a weapon in case of an emergency. Usually, the first thing that comes to mind is the "Wolverine" method, where we put a key between our knuckles. The problem with this method is that we have to be very close to an attacker to use it (not ideal), and if not held properly, the keys can hurt your hand or slide around as you're trying to defend yourself with them. Plus, as smart entry and keyless fobs become more common, we may not even be carrying any keys to use this method.

Instead, experts recommend that we carry other self-defense tools on our key rings, like mini flashlights, anti-wolf defense tools (or kubotans), personal alarms, whistles, or lanyards that can turn your keys into makeshift nunchucks if needed. You don't need to have all of these items on your keys, but they're small enough that if you wanted to have them all, you could, and since they're on your keys, you'll know you'll always have them with you. Let's break down a few of these items and their uses:

- **Mini flashlight:** I've lived in NYC for nearly ten years, and I don't know how many times I've gotten stuck in a subway tunnel. A mini flashlight was something I always kept on me in case I needed to trek through a tunnel to get to a platform or if I simply needed the light to find something in my purse.

- **Kubotan or anti-wolf defense tool:** When you're looking this up online, sometimes it's listed as an anti-wolf defense tool or a kubotan. Essentially, it's a self-defense weapon often made of aluminum that's put on a key chain and can be used in a variety of emergency situations. It can be used to jab or stab at a bad guy or even break a window or other type of glass in an emergency (it doesn't work well on car windows, however). Having a stick like a kubotan on your key chain is also helpful if you need to use your keys as a line of defense. It'll provide you with some distance so you can swing your keys like nunchucks. Please note these are typically not allowed in airports or in government buildings, so keep that in mind as you travel or run errands.

- **Personal alarms:** To help deter an attack, many people carry personal alarms. They're high-decibel alarms that usually have a flashing strobe light on them as well. (They're often pretty cute too. They can look like hearts or kitties or just a colorful key chain.) The louder the better. The concept behind these alarms is that the shrill sound might send someone running, but they're also a way to call for help, since most of them are so loud they can be heard from a hundred feet away. They're also easy to use, making them accessible for people with disabilities, seniors, and even young kids. Also, while many states have laws about pepper spray and stun guns, personal alarms are generally legal everywhere, so they're easy to pack in a suitcase when you travel.

- **A whistle:** Similar to the personal alarm, a whistle is also used to ward off unwanted attention or to call for help in the case of an emergency. The difference is that it requires you to be physically able to blow the whistle, while a personal alarm will usually emit a signal on its own for as long as the battery lasts. For those moments when the battery is dead or you simply want another option, a whistle is an easy item that you can also toss in your bag when you're traveling.

- **A lanyard, chain, or carabiner:** Having a lanyard or a carabiner on your key chain is handy for a variety of reasons, but they can also be used for self-defense. If you need to swing at someone, you'll have much more distance between yourself and the person; plus, if you're grabbed, you can still keep swinging. It easier to defend yourself this way and more effective.

GTFO wrist strap or bracelet: I learned about this tool from a viral TikTok video. It's a lightweight, adjustable, and discreet bracelet with a tungsten carbide striker bead. It was originally created for people in high-risk capture situations like government officials or military personnel, but it has uses for the general public, like helping you break out of a vehicle in an emergency situation. The bracelet is elastic and easy to use. If you remember making mini slingshots with rubber bands in between your fingers as a kid, it's the same concept. You hold the bracelet like a slingshot in your hand and let the tungsten bead hit the glass you're trying to break. Some of these bracelets are also sold with pins built into them, which could get you out of handcuffs if needed. As an alternative, many survivalists recommend carrying a bobby pin with you, because they can also be used to escape handcuffs or pick a lock if needed.

Mirrors and reflective sunglasses: One thing I always like to carry in my purse is a mirror or sunglasses. I do this so that if I feel like I'm being followed, I can pretend to put on some lipstick or clean my sunglasses and use them to get a better look at who's behind me. I've actually used this tactic in real life. In the early aughts in New York City, I was walking along Avenue B when a man started walking behind me and picking up pace. I wasn't sure if his eyes were on me or if he was trying to pass me on the sidewalk, so I used my sunglasses to look behind me and kept walking. As he got closer, he started saying something that I don't remember, but I do remember being scared. I was barely a teenager. My aunt had taught me to never look scared when you're approached and walk fast but not in a way that seems unnatural; stay cool and collected but make an exit. That's exactly what I did, and eventually the man hung back, and soon I was out of his range. I didn't have any other tools on me at that time except for sunglasses and a mirror, which I kept using to check the distance between me and the man who was making me uncomfortable.

Battery pack: As great as our phones are, the battery life sometimes leaves a lot to be desired. There are battery packs small enough to fit on a key chain, some are built into phone cases, and then there are the ones large enough to charge our phones for days and even jump-start a car. Especially if you take public transit or if you're going out for a long night, there's nothing worse than a phone with a low battery. It sucks for a ton of reasons, but safety is certainly on that list. If you're sharing your location, wearing a smart safety device, or using a safety app, none of that will work if your phone is dead.

Purse hook: Keeping valuables like your purse in your line of sight helps prevent theft. Instead of hanging your purse on the back of a chair or putting it on the floor (which is also bad luck), a purse hook keeps everything visible so that sneaky hands will have a harder time and hopefully move on.

Mini first aid items: You may not want to carry a full first aid kit in your purse, but if you can slip in two adhesive bandages, a travel pack of painkillers, and a mini hand sanitizer, you'll be covered for the minor inconveniences like the shoe that's causing a blister or the pounding headache. Now that we've learned to live with COVID-19, I think we'll be singing the praises of hand sanitizer for decades to come, so I trust you've got that handy already.

Routines: Having a routine is nice—we like consistency—but a retired FBI agent once told me that while he was trained to switch up his routine for safety, he's always been surprised that it's not a common practice among the public. It's easy to always take the same route to work or school or even walking the dog, but predictability is also a risk. If I know that you live alone and every morning at eight you go for a two-mile run, then I know that every morning at eight, your home is empty. I may also know the exact route you run. Depending on our lifestyle, switching up our routines could be as simple as changing the road we take a couple of times a week. Maybe it's not something we think about all the time until that creep at the park makes a comment that rubs us the wrong way. Whatever the reason may be, know that changing your routine is a good safety habit.

Your gut instinct: This is the best tool out there. Obviously this isn't something you can buy in a store but, luckily, it's an aspect of self that I believe we're all born with, and arguably the best safety tool in your kit. We have an innate ability to take note of what's around us and decide whether we're in a safe situation. Over time we may dull this instinct by telling ourselves we're overreacting and there's no reason we should feel creeped out by that nice man in the park, but I believe our senses pick up things before we're able to verbalize them.

Situational awareness: Most of the content in this book can be summed up by these two words: situational awareness. Simply put, situational awareness is the effort to identify, process, and understand what is happening around us, while thinking ahead so we can prevent or mitigate a safety threat. When we're in our daily zone, distracted by our phones or music, it's easy to tune out what's going on around us, but that's an incredibly vulnerable place to be in. Taking a moment to look around, see who's behind us, and be aware can help us make better safety predictions about our environments. While grocery shopping, do you know where the emergency exits are? If there's an emergency, knowing where the exits are and the fastest route to get to them can save you valuable time in trying to get to safety.

Situational awareness helps us be alert, which makes us less of a target, but it also helps us understand what normal looks like so that we can better recognize what's not normal and react accordingly. It doesn't mean you're always walking around in a heightened state of anxiety—there are stages. You can be relaxed but aware and alert. That level of alertness gets heightened when you notice something doesn't look or feel right. You may not act on your observation, but you are prepared to react if needed. The most heightened form of awareness is when you're actually concerned for your safety because there's a threat.

For example, you walk into a doctor's office, and everyone is relaxed, waiting to be called, but there's one person who's alone, visibly anxious, he's got his hand in a jacket pocket, and he's shaking. Is he acting this way because he's terrified of the doctor or because he's planning something malicious? Your gut instinct will tell you where to position your level of alertness and whether you should report what you're seeing, get yourself away from the situation, or both.

Here are a few ways you can start practicing situational awareness today:

- **Avoid autopilot:** When using electronics, don't let them drown out what's around you. Only use one earbud or keep the volume low so that you can still hear what's happening close by. The same is true if you're reading a book on public transit or studying at a library—don't let yourself get so in the zone that you're completely unaware of what's happening nearby.

- **Head on a swivel:** Look around you and use your peripheral vision. Also, use items around you to increase your visibility. For example, reflective surfaces like sunglasses, a window, a black television or laptop screen, or even a windshield can all be used as ways to look around you.

- **Quick scan:** Where are the exits? Are there barriers? Who's in the area? Anyone acting out of the ordinary? Scan your environment, whether it's new or the coffee shop you visit every day.

- **Plan a route:** In the case of an emergency, what are your exit options? This applies while you're on foot but also when you're driving or taking public transportation.
  Like many New Yorkers, I relied on public transportation when I lived and worked in the city. Sometimes there were storms, which I knew could shut down the subway, and because no one likes being stuck in a

subway car, I'd adjust my route and take a bus instead. It would take longer, often double the time of taking the subway, but worst-case scenario, I knew I'd have more control over when I walked off a bus than I would have getting off a subway car. Plus, if I got stuck in a subway car, there was no guarantee my cellphone would work. It may not always be a feasible option to change your route, but thinking about the possibilities ahead of time can help you avoid an uncomfortable situation.

- **Watch your back:** Ideally, you want to be able to see what's around you, but you also don't want to be backed into a corner. Having your back to a wall where you can move left, right, or forward is fine, but you don't want to put yourself in a position where you have only one exit that can easily be blocked. You can practice avoiding being backed into a corner at restaurants, at a bus stop, and even when driving or parking.

- **Personal space:** One of the benefits of living through COVID-19 is that people have become hyperaware of personal space. Five to six feet is ideal for giving you room to react, so if someone's giving you a creepy vibe, resort to COVID rules and give yourself some distance.

- **See something, say something:** Wherever you are, if you see something suspicious or feel that something is suspicious, report it to the proper authorities. But while this is incredibly important and can even save lives, it's also important we do this responsibly. We can't let hidden biases color our interpretation of what's happening around us, and we shouldn't escalate an uncomfortable situation. If someone's in a hoodie in the middle of a heat wave or waiting by the back exit of an apartment building at two a.m., that might call for further investigation. If a car has been abandoned by a park or you notice a suspicious package, certainly it's worth reporting, but if someone is having a picnic in a park with their children, that scenario shouldn't raise red flags unless they're also accompanied by weapons. Practicing situational awareness is one way to observe what's normal so that we can get in tune with our gut and recognize suspicious behavior.

These are some steps you can think about, but ultimately, only you will know how to exercise situational awareness best in your environment. It's a tool we all have access to, it's free, and it takes little skill to start implementing. It may take some conscious effort at first, but eventually it will become a habit.

Self-defense courses: Tools are great, but even better is taking some time to invest in a self-defense course. As a little kid, I started martial arts to help give me the confidence to fight off a school bully. I stuck with it until high school. At that time, it was more about having fun with my friends, getting that black belt, and easy exercise, but as I got older, I realized there was more value in those courses than I had considered. I learned how to defend myself with simple moves like bending a finger, which can bring someone to the ground in seconds. (And no, I didn't break any fingers—just bent them!) Learning martial arts helped my reflexes, taught me how to be aware of my surroundings, and taught me how not to fight. In my courses, we learned how to de-escalate situations and how to get away, but never to instigate. Self-defense is always a last resort, and it's an incredibly valuable skill to have.

Martial arts are a great activity for all ages, and there are courses that cater to a variety of physical abilities. Also, while I took classes for years, you don't have to do that. There are weekend workshops and online courses, and many college campuses, schools, and law enforcement agencies also offer courses. One well-known program offered throughout the United States, as well as in Canada, Egypt, the United Kingdom, and Switzerland, is called R.A.D. Systems. They offer courses for women, men, seniors, and kids. If you're in an area outside their network or want to learn about other programs offered nearby, check with your local schools, community centers, and law enforcement agencies for recommendations.

Listen to your gut: Ultimately, the best thing you can carry with you is a tuned-in gut feeling. If you feel uncomfortable around someone, there's a reason for that. If your children feel uncomfortable around someone, there's a reason for it. If you're handed a drink and suddenly have a nagging feeling telling you not to drink it, there's a reason. Listen to your gut.

If you're a true-crime junkie, you've probably heard countless crime stories with victims saying something along the lines of "I had an uneasy feeling when [insert incident], but I didn't want to make a big deal of it" or "Looking back, I realized something was weird." Maybe you have your own stories. I think we can all think of a moment when our gut told us something and we ignored it or when we listened and were grateful. I can think of several in my own life—some serious, some not so much. I'll share a small example.

I was in fifth grade, and it was one of the few days my mom let me walk home alone from school. I basically lived across the street, so it was an easy walk. As I approached the street to cross, I waited for the cars to pass. One car stopped in the middle of the street and the driver gestured with his arm. It looked like he was calling me over to his car. I gestured my hand as if to say, "No, you go ahead," but then he gestured again, and it grew more urgent. We went back and forth twice. He wasn't driving off, so I ran back to school and called my mom to pick me up. In hindsight, I think he was gesturing for me to cross the street, but his insistence on my crossing when I had already said no, paired with the fact that no one else was around, scared me. It's possible he was simply a kind man who wanted to make sure a child crossed the road safely, but that was a high-stakes bet I wasn't willing to place. It was less risky to listen to my gut and call my mom. Plus, I didn't want this random stranger knowing what neighborhood I lived in. These were the calculations I made in my ten-year-old head during a fifteen-second nonverbal conversation.

I mention this childhood story because I believe our gut safety instincts are innate. That nagging feeling that warns us of danger is within us already, but it's up to us to nurture it. When I was five or ten, I wasn't consciously nurturing my instincts, but when I look back and remember the times I listened versus the times I didn't, one major lesson stands out: when I listened, I was protected.

Listening to your gut might seem like a difficult task, but in reality, you're probably doing it. We interact with complete strangers every day. Maybe it's during a food delivery or a date, or with people at work, riders on the train, or people at school. We're around people all the time, but it's unlikely you have a nagging feeling telling you you're in danger every second of the day. Why is that? Why aren't we walking around in constant fear? Could it be because we're taking clues from our environment, from the behaviors we see, and from patterns we've recognized in order to assess what's high-risk? That's definitely true for me, so before you start doubting yourself or wondering if you're intuitive enough, remember that you're already doing it and have likely been doing it for years. Bottom line: trust yourself.

Confidence: When we're alone for a walk, bike ride, or run, we might seem like an easy target. Despite all the tools we have to help in the case of a crime, another hidden tool to prevent a crime is confidence. Police have warned that something as simple as posture can make a difference when a potential attacker is scoping out their next victim. I don't want our minds to always go to the worst, but whether it's a violent criminal or a street pickpocket, carrying ourselves with confidence can deter a potential threat. When you're out and about, keep your head up, shoulders back, and walk with power. If you seem distracted or afraid, you're more likely to become a target.

Also, when we're acting on our gut feelings and telling someone to get away from us, our confidence needs to roar. Having confidence isn't only how we carry ourselves but also how we prepare for those moments. For example, if you're going for a bike ride, do you know your route? Do you have a phone so you can call for help? Are you staying on familiar paths or well-lit, populated paths? Did you tell someone you were going for a ride? Taking steps like these can help us feel more confident when we're out so we don't have to fake it. That said, if you have to fake it, then fake it.

Ever wonder why street scam artists can always pick out the tourist from the crowd? They're good at reading people, but being confident and blending in throws them off their game. So go ahead and let your light shine. Not only are you absolutely worthy but it's a safety precaution as well.

Situations When It's Best to Lie

My most popular video series by far is *Situations When It's Best to Lie*. On those posts, I share everyday questions that could be low-key manipulative and even dangerous so my viewers can see real-life examples of times when they shouldn't tell the truth. This series was inspired by a trip to the grocery store when I encountered a very friendly cashier. As I was checking out, the cashier was making conversation and started recommending restaurants nearby. Then he stopped to ask, "Where do you live?" I knew his intent was to gauge my location so he could make better recommendations, so I didn't shut him down and instead responded with a quick "Oh, I'm just down the road." What road? He'll never know because I was intentionally vague, and, frankly, he could make recommendations without knowing exactly where I lived. It was an innocuous conversation at a checkout counter, but it reminded me of some training I had received while hosting shows on a national television network.

During my onboarding, I was warned about fans—fans who, like the grocery clerk, might ask seemingly innocent but uncomfortable questions such as where I lived. I was prepared with a bunch of vague responses I could call on should the situation ever come up, and the moment that grocery clerk inquired, I was reminded of my training. Those videos have received millions of views—the most popular was viewed more than thirty-three million times on my account, but it was reposted so many times by media outlets all over the world that the impact was much greater than my little TikTok page.

This series isn't a perfect formula. If you're at the bank and they ask for your address to open an account, it's perfectly reasonable to provide them with that information. If you're asked where you live for a job application or a school loan, these are likely harmless situations. But if you're at a bus stop or traveling on a plane and the passenger sitting next to you starts asking you where you live, that's when your little red flag should go up. If I'm enjoying the conversation and my red flag goes up, I continue chatting but use one of my go-to vague responses. In nine out of ten cases, the person continues on as usual, but if the person catches on to the fact that I'm being vague and becomes persistent, then my gut morphs into a cheerleading squad of red flags and I quickly make an exit.

All right, so let's talk about some of these common questions and some easy vague responses you can use:

Where do you live?
- "I'm just down the road."
- "Fifteen minutes down the road."

- "I'm in town."
- "By the Walmart" (or any chain with a ton of locations nearby).
- If your area has a ton of corporate apartments, you can mention the name of one of the big companies. For example, AvalonBay Communities is the third largest owner of apartments in the United States. Depending on where you're located, saying you live at the Avalon can be super vague. That conversation could look something like this:

> *"Where do you live?"*
> *"Do you know the Avalon? Gorgeous apartments."*
> *"Oh, not really, but maybe you can pick a place nearby for a drink?"*

Did you lie? Eh . . . you misled, but you didn't really lie. Until you trust this person, they don't need to know where you live.

Where do you work?
- "At the electric company."
- "I'm in marketing/advertising/sales/communications" (all super vague).
- "Oh, I'm remote."
- "I freelance."
- "I'm in finance—you know how that is. . . ."

Does anyone else live with you? Do you live alone?
(Examples of who might ask you these questions are a repairman making conversation, a taxicab driver, or a nosy neighbor.)
- "Yes, and I'm actually having some guests soon."
- "Yeah; my roommate had to report to the military base today, but he'll be back soon."
- "Yeah; I have roommates."

- "My husband's in the shower" (you can even run the shower or a bathroom vent to make this sound legit).

The roommate lie works best if you're not in your home, or, if you are, when the doors to the bedrooms are shut. The bottom line is that if someone is prying, don't admit to being alone. Some people even go as far as to call out "I'll get the door" when going to accept a food delivery or yelling "Babe, I'm back" when they get home so that neighbors won't know they live alone.

Are you meeting friends?
- "Yep—that's where I'm headed."

Going home alone?
- "Nope—going to a friend's house."
- "No. I'm heading to my dad's house."

You're going out alone tonight?
- "No. My friends are waiting for me."

Where do you go to school?
- "At home."
- "It's online, so I get to pick a new spot for school every day."

Traveling alone?
- "Nope. Waiting for a friend."
- "No. I have family here."
- "No; my friends are a few rows back" (if on a plane, bus, or train).

When do you work?
- "I don't know—my boss is always changing the schedule."
- "I just fill in when they need me."

- "It's not a consistent schedule."
- "I couldn't say. It changes every week."

Is this your car?
- "It's borrowed."

Where are you headed next?
- "A doctor's appointment."
- "My dad's house."
- "My boyfriend's house."
- "My brother's house."
- "My friend's house. They just returned from a military tour."

Do you need a ride?
- "No, thank you. I have family picking me up."
- "No; my friends are just a few minutes away."

Note that in many airports, it's illegal for strangers to offer rides.

Do you know people in town?
- "Yeah; I have friends in town."
- "Yes. I used to live here."
- "My family is in town."

Is it your first time visiting?
- "No. I used to live here" (works best if you're familiar with the area).

Are you staying at this hotel?
- "No. I'm waiting for a friend."

Where are you staying?
- "The Marriott."

It's the world's largest hotel chain, with more than eight thousand hotels in sixty-six countries, and they likely have multiple locations within the same city, so it's kind of hard to pin down the exact hotel. (That said, you know the places around your home best, so if there's another prominent chain in your area, use that.)

Is this your first time traveling?

- "Nope."

You're never a newbie. You're always a pro who's done this a thousand times. Unless you're getting help from a flight attendant, no one needs to know how familiar you are with the airport.

Are you working alone?

- "No. My boss is in the back."
- "No. There are always at least two of us here."

What dorm are you in?

- "I commute."

Are you a first year?

- "Do I look like one?"

Can you let me into the building?

- "No."

So many thefts, or worse, have begun because someone let a stranger into the building. Protect yourself and your neighbors by getting comfortable with saying no.

Is this your first time here?

- "Does it look like it?"
- "No, I've been here before."

Tone is important here. Think about what response you hope to elicit before you answer.

Do you play sports here?

- "Not really."

Sports rosters at many schools are public, so if someone's being creepy, you may not want them to be able to look you up.

Can I get your number?

- "Sorry, not interested."
- "Sure"—[looks at watch]—"oh shoot; I'm late. I gotta run."
- "That's flattering, but I'm married."
- "Why? Why? Why?"
- "Why don't you give me yours?"
- "I can give you my parole officer's number . . ."
- Or you can use a digital number like Google Voice for these situations.

Where do you do yoga?

- "Just on YouTube."

Do you work out here?

- "Just trying it for the day."

Do you live in the building?

- "Nope. Just visiting."
- "No. Just visiting my dad [or boyfriend]."

Are your parents home?

- "Yeah; they're on a work call. Leave your information at the door."
- "Yes. Why?"
- "They're upstairs, so leave your message at the door and I'll have them get it later."

These questions seem innocent, and maybe they are—but if you don't know the person asking, how can you know their intent? Let your gut guide you, and if you need a go-to lie, feel free to borrow from one of the examples above.

Ordering a cab: Especially if you're ordering from a location that you frequent, I suggest using a nearby address, like the intersection of two streets. Additionally, if you ever feel uncomfortable when you're in a cab or other scenario and need someone to know that people are tracking you, you can save a fake call to your phone. There are a ton of videos online that you can save if you want to fake a speakerphone conversation, but you can also simply pick up the phone and pretend to have a conversation on your own. Maybe it could sound something like this:

"Dad? Yes, I know. I'm on my way. . . . Dad, I'll be there in five minutes. You don't have to track me. . . . All right, fine—I'll stay on the phone with you."

Ordering takeout: When ordering takeout via an app or online, use your initials instead of your full name so the delivery person can't guess your gender, or use a nickname (preferably one that's gender neutral). A lot of people also opt for a masculine-sounding name.

Being approached: Sometimes you're approached and need a quick exit. Depending on the timing, you can pretend you got freaked out by a bug or that you don't notice the person as you fidget with your umbrella and walk away—or, of course, you can pretend to be busy talking on the phone. You can also develop a list of go-to responses such as:

- "I'm running late, gotta go."
- "Sorry, I'm busy at the moment."
- "*Perdon, estoy apurada*" (What's that? You're suddenly bilingual? Yes, baddie!).

Knowing another language has its perks, one of them being that you can get out of conversations you don't want to have by simply pretending not to speak the local language. If you happen to choose a language the nosy stranger also speaks, then turn to another easy conversational exit like the ones above, or pretend that you have an incoming call. And if all else fails, fake the crazy. If someone's standing too close and creeping you out and nothing else seems to work, get crazy. Yell or make big gestures. Chances are you'll freak them out and they'll back off. You can also pretend to know someone around you. When you address someone in this way, they'll usually play along and help you get out of the uncomfortable situation.

It's important to note that every scenario is different and you should trust your gut. Only you will know the best response for the situation. For example, if you're at a dog park, you might find yourself talking with strangers about your pets. Context matters, and remember that part of someone's decision about whether to approach you may depend on your body language. If you're looking down at your phone or reading and not making eye contact with anyone, it's unlikely anyone will approach you to chat.

While we're on the subject of warding off unwanted advances, here are a few more scenarios:

YOUR VOICE MAIL

You don't need to personalize it. There's nothing wrong with the default robotic voice, but if you do choose to personalize it, one option is to have a friend or loved one with a deep voice resembling a dad's record the message for you.

You don't have to give someone your real phone number every time you're asked. Whether it's the grocery store reward program, the flirtatious bartender, or someone who wants to connect for a networking opportunity, I repeat: *you don't have to give them your real phone number.* Our phone numbers are connected to so much information—from social media profiles to people-finder websites—that we should be protective of them. Instead of giving your real phone number, give a number from an internet-based service like Google Voice. And by the way, another way to protect your phone number is to ask your carrier if you can set up an extra layer of security like a PIN or passcode. This is similar to two-factor authentication, which we'll talk about in the next chapter.

TEXTING AND FAKING AN AUTO RESPONSE

When you get unsolicited explicit photos via text or email, you can ignore them, block the sender, or pull out one of the auto responses below that will make the person think twice before sending something else:

These suggestions aren't necessarily for safety's sake but are more focused on getting the person to reflect on what they've sent. I'll add that in most cases it's safest to disengage. Maybe you have a Petty Betty moment, but you don't want a small prank to escalate.

> This is an automated message generated by the [enter social media platform or cell phone service provider] team. Your image has been found to be a violation of policy and was flagged as harassment. Your account is scheduled for further reporting.

> Auto response: Thank you for your submission to our photo essay. Your name and photos will be published shortly.

CHAPTER 3

CYBERSECURITY: THINGS YOU SHOULDN'T POST AND PROTECTING YOUR DATA

A Little Privacy, Please

I'm very active on social media and spend a lot of time online. I shop online, I bank online, I use smart-home devices regularly. I love technology. I'm never going to be the person who suggests living off the grid in the name of cybersecurity, but I do encourage operating online with full awareness. What does that mean? Well, with a sense of awareness we can assess risk and make informed decisions. Awareness is an empowering tool for anyone who values safety and security.

Unfortunately, some of the greatest risks for our safety happen online, and cybersecurity is one of the topics we aren't taught in school—at least not yet. There's no universal "Stranger Danger Cybersecurity" campaign in elementary schools or "Click It or Ticket"–inspired highway signs warning people of the dangers of oversharing online. Unless an incident of hacking or identity theft or the like ends up in the news or happens to a friend, we probably don't think much about it. We've all read about social media platforms being hacked, but has it impacted our online habits? Eh . . . probably not. If you do as little as change your passwords on a semiregular basis, you're already light-years ahead of the game. Which isn't a great sign for the rest of us.

And the risk doesn't end with online scammers or identity theft—it actually gets worse. Yep, that's right: digital stalking is definitely a danger. Before we all spent so much time online, someone would need to be physically nearby to stalk you, but now they can do it from anywhere in the world. Many of us have done this innocently when checking someone out before a first date or researching a candidate we're looking to hire— these are not necessarily malicious actions, but in the wrong hands, it can become dangerous. Perhaps there's an obsessed ex, a superfan, a toxic friend you cut ties with, or someone who's trolling you because they don't like a comment you posted online—there are a ton of reasons why someone may have malicious intent toward you or your loved ones, so here are some ways to protect your information while also being able to stay online and be public.

THE PRIVATE PROFILE

Undoubtedly, the best way to stay private is to have private social media profiles. It's not a guarantee the information will stay private, so you still need to be cautious about what you post, but it's a way to keep your circle tight. You can easily mix it up too—your Facebook can be private, while your Instagram is public, and that can determine what information you share on each profile.

WHAT'S YOUR HANDLE?

Depending on your career, you can make your social media handles and usernames obscure. A handle like @BlueElephants or @user12345 doesn't tell anyone much about the person running that account, and if they're not posting identifying factors, it's even harder to figure out their identity. That being said, if you are someone who needs to be public for work—think real estate agents, journalists, entertainers— you may need to have a social media profile with your name included, in which case you have to be more cautious with what, when, and how you post online. You can also have multiple accounts, keeping some things private and others public.

ASK ME ANYTHING . . .

I share a ton! On any given day I might post ten Instagram stories and a TikTok. I pretty much spend most of my day on social media, so I understand wanting to share aspects of your life online, but let's establish a list of things to consider before posting. These rules can help keep you and your information safe from prying eyes.

- **Don't overshare:** It should almost go without saying, but don't share any sensitive information. That means no credit card numbers, debit card PINs, verification codes, social security numbers, ultrasound scans with your legal name and your doctor's name, college acceptance letters revealing student details—none of that. You can share your accomplishments and milestones without including a photograph of highly sensitive information. There may be times when you want to post some of this, like an ultrasound photo or your first car, but take a few moments to obscure the sensitive details before sharing.

- **Don't post in real time:** Watch the timing of your posts. You do not need to post what you're doing in the exact moment you're doing it. You can post those vacation photos once you're back. You can post about the great food after you've left the restaurant or tag the show after you've left the theater. There is no rule that says everything you post has to be in real time.

    It seems simple enough, but it's a mistake I've seen even A-list celebs make. Years ago, I was in New York City's West Village scrolling through Instagram while on my way to a salon. I noticed a celeb had posted that she was at a popular restaurant in the area, and I was one block away. As I walked past the restaurant, I peeked in, and sure enough, she was at the bar of the restaurant. I couldn't believe the risk she had taken. What if I were an obsessed fan or someone with malicious intent? I don't know if she was aware of the risk she had taken by sharing where she was eating. The truth is, if she had waited until she left the restaurant to post her meal, would it have affected her content? Would the restaurant have seemed any less cool? Probably not. Would she have been safer? Almost certainly yes.

- **Watch for photobombs:** Pay attention to what's behind you when you're snapping a selfie. Can I see your address or apartment number? Are you regularly posting from the same train station? Can I see the name of your school or workplace? Is that your license plate or a sticker on the back of your car that tells me what school you go to? What about packages? Can I zoom in and see an address? Or, worse, is the address prominently displayed in an unboxing video?

These little details get overlooked a lot, but they're important to remember, particularly in our offices (whether those are at home or in another location). You may have student records on your desk or sensitive company information all out in the open, and if you're not paying attention when you post a photo of your fancy morning coffee, you may make that information public.

Several years ago, I saw a celeb post a photo of her kids sitting on the back of her car, with her license plate visible. She had just been cast on a big national show, so she only had about eight thousand followers at the time, but I immediately DMed her to let her know that was risky. I may have creeped her out, but she did take down the photo.

When you're scrolling through social media, take notice of how often you see this. I've come across viral Tik-Tok videos where people have their full driver's license facing the camera because of the way they're holding their wallets. I've also seen where a woman posted on LinkedIn that she had bought a new home, and she was standing right next to the house number for hundreds of thousands of people to see online.

In many cases, nothing happens, but this sort of visibility speaks to the need for awareness. When showing off your cute OOTD, why does your driver's license need to be in the picture? Or your work ID? It takes seconds to simply adjust your angle or remove the item. And if your intent is to show off the car or ID, blur the details before sharing.

- **Check reflective surfaces:** Watch what's reflected on surfaces in your photos. It can lead to some pretty embarrassing moments. A few years ago, a celeb accidentally posted a nude because she didn't realize her body was reflected in the packaging of a product she was promoting. Whether it's a mirror, the television, your dark laptop screen, plastic wrap, sunglasses, or even your bathtub faucet in that cute photo of your bubble bath, pay attention to what's reflected.

- **To geotag or not?** A geotag is metadata that reveals where you took a photo, and it's available on most social media apps. It's not always a bad thing; sometimes you want to share the location of the coffee shop you found or that landmark you visited, but what if that geotag is your house? To give yourself control over this feature, turn off automatic geotagging in your settings. You'll have to look up how to do it on each platform, but typically it's under the "Privacy and Security" tab. Once the geotagging is turned off, you can still tag your photos, but you'll be able to choose what you want the tag to say and how broad of an area you want to tag.

- **Tagging friends and businesses:** When tagging a photo, whether it's a geotag or the people, think about what you're tagging. If you spend most of your time at work, you may not want to tag your workplace's location. The same goes for the gym. And if you're tagging friends, consider how they approach posting. Is their profile public? Are they careful too? Because if you're trying to remain private but tag your best friend, who overshares and is public, then someone could go to their page to learn more about you and your whereabouts.

  If privacy is important to you, think about who you're tagging, what you are tagging, and how revealing that information is. You can always skip the tagging altogether, unless you're sharing someone's content and need to credit them.

- **You have it, but do you want to flaunt it?** This is a gray area and will vary depending on what kind of content you post. But before you post valuables, consider the risks. If you don't want people to know you have thousands of dollars of luxury goods, don't post about them, and if you are going to post, maybe skip sharing where you store these things. I love a good house tour or closet tour—after all, we all love to see how celebs live—but in some cases, sharing what you have, how much of it you have, and where you keep it could be risky.

- **Viral trend caution:** I'm all for a viral trend, but hopping on some of them can overexpose our information. If a trend is asking you to post anything that could be used to figure out your passwords or answer password-recovery questions, do not post that. They may seem innocent at first, but if they start asking you to reveal your favorite teacher growing up, your favorite book, or your dog's nickname, then skip it. General quizzes about what your favorite animal says about you or what type of cheese fits best with your personality are fine. But look out for those chain posts that ask you for personal details.

In addition to the cybersecurity risks, some trends are simply revealing. You may recall the silhouette challenge on social media a few years ago where a red light would cover a sexy silhouetted body. Within days, the internet was manipulating the videos to remove the red filter that gave the images anonymity, and people had revealed more of their bodies than they initially intended. The trend was so popular that it ended up in a beer commercial, but for people who participated in the trend nude, their privacy was violated in a very intimate way.

- **The safety-first OOTD:** The group photo, bathroom selfie, or mirror picture is cute until you realize you're wearing your ID around your neck in the photo.

  When I worked at a national television network, all employees were told not to take photos in their work lanyards. The concern was that someone following an employee's social media page could use these images to make their own version of our company IDs and pose as an employee in the building. To my knowledge, it hadn't happened, but our team of experts wanted that precaution in place. It's a good habit to get into.

  If you're not at work or school, take off your ID. Whether you're posting a photo online or riding public transit, having your ID on is needless extra information (plus, it ruins the outfit). It's also best to take off the ID instead of blurring it out, but if it's going to be in the picture, use an eraser tool or a blur tool to cover it. Another popular method is to use emojis to cover private information, but, depending on how the image is shared, there are tools online that can remove an emoji from a photo. If you mainly post on social media, then an emoji, a blur tool, or a combination of both is a good go-to.

And for my athletes: if you're on a school team and walk around with a backpack or shirt that displays your college and team number, keep in mind that many sports rosters are public. Remember that the next time you post that selfie in your jersey.

- **What's in your screenshot?** Whether it's your work conference, virtual classroom, or virtual happy hour, when we're not physically together, the only way of sharing these moments is to take a screenshot—but before sharing, take a look at what's actually in the screenshot. Is everyone's full legal name visible? If so, maybe you can edit that before posting or adjust settings before snapping the picture. Also, consider the privacy of others who may be in the virtual room with you—some people are more private than others, so when in doubt, err on the side of caution and edit the information.

- **Are minors in the photo/video?** This is a tip I learned when I worked in television. I frequently worked with public figures, some of whom were targets of stalking, and there was always a concern about how this stalking could affect their children. We were told not to post photos of the faces of our children, particularly older ones who have established features.

    Most people ignore this tip; it's simply too difficult not

to share photos of your family. I totally get it. I certainly follow my share of cute family accounts, but there are instances when no matter who you are, you should be cautious. Dating profiles are a good example. It's okay to say you're a parent, but you don't need to post photos of your children for strangers to see. You can blur their faces, but it's probably best to skip it altogether and simply say you're a parent in the bio. Similarly, when you're selling used items online, skip the family photo as your profile picture. The person buying your old coffee pot doesn't need to know how many kids you have, their ages, or what they look like.

There you have it: the Mom Friend list of cybersecurity best practices. Bonus points if you add some rules of your own, but I hope this serves as a good place to start. Do I actually think about all this stuff when I post to my millions of followers online? Yes, I do. I don't spend hours analyzing every post, but I keep these things in mind, and I always take a few seconds of my time to adjust. Sometimes I break a rule or best practice, but only after I've considered the risks and decided that I was willing to take the gamble; that's the differentiator. If someone doesn't know they've put themselves at risk, it feels like a violation. Knowing something is a risk and choosing to ignore it is much more empowering than unknowingly posting details you wouldn't want public.

Cybersecurity: Ways to Protect Your Data

What we post isn't the only way our data ends up available to the public. There are data breaches that can leak our emails, passwords, or phone numbers for hackers and scammers to take advantage of—almost everyone is aware of these risks. But another danger is data brokers who collect our personal information from a variety of sources, list it publicly for anyone to find online, and sell data as well. It's invasive and could be dangerous, not only because of scammers who can use this information to add validity to their scams but also in terms of personal safety.

If you had a bad date, upset someone online, or have someone who's just obsessed with you, they can easily access this information on a whim. Unfortunately, as of this writing, the responsibility to monitor all this data falls on us if we live in the US.

Here are some of my favorite tools and best practices for protecting your data. Keep in mind none of these are foolproof. Even with all of these tools in place, you can still get hacked, fall victim to a phishing scam, or have someone find your details online, but it's good to know what resources are available to you if you want to regain some control over your data.

SEARCH FOR YOURSELF ON
ALL THE MAJOR SEARCH ENGINES

It's likely someone will search for you online at some point, so why not do it before they do? Maybe it's while you're hunting for a new job, applying to college, or starting to date, but someone has probably typed your name into a search engine, and you've probably done the same for someone else.

People are shocked by how much information is available with a quick click of a button. Every time you order something online, take out a loan, buy a house, change an address, or go to a bank, companies are collecting data from you, and they use that data for marketing, advertising, and other purposes, which is how some of your information ends up being public without your consent or knowledge. Your phone number, name, age, address, email, and relatives' names are likely all available online. It's unsettling, and, unfortunately, something you have to keep track of, because no one else is going to do it for you. Pro tip: search yourself monthly.

How to get started

1. In a search engine, search your name in quotation marks. If there are too many results, you may need to go through several pages before finding yourself. You can also add modifiers like your city or state to get more specific results.

2. Search for your email addresses, social media handles, phone numbers, street addresses (prior and current), and relatives' names. If your information pops up on people-finding websites such as whitepages.com, mylife.com, spokeo.com, or intelius.com (there are many more), you can likely get it taken down by contacting the websites directly. Many of them have online forms you can submit to get your information removed or a phone number you can call.

3. Don't forget images! When you type in your information, images of you will pop up, and if anything is concerning, you can do a reverse image search to find out where the image is being hosted and hopefully get it taken down. Google also allows you to request that certain images be removed from their search results, but there are some contraints. If you search "Google remove an image request," you'll find their support page to walk you through the steps and limitations.

4. Use the OpenSource Intelligence or OSINT framework. Aside from searching directly for your information in a search engine, you can use websites that are already harvesting this information, such as maltego.com, spiderfoot.net, and osintframework.com. These websites have a bit of a learning curve, but they're excellent research tools you can use to hunt down where some of your information may be hiding. That said, if they start

feeling too techie, default to looking up your information in various search engines.

5. For more techniques on how to find information, you can also look up "Google dorking." It's a method for using symbols or words to get more precise search results, and it can be used to track down your information on a variety of search engines.

What to do once you've found the information

1. Try to avoid clicking on the link from the search results page in the search engine. Instead, try to find your listing directly on the company website. Some common websites include Intelius, Spokeo, and Whitepages, as well as wedding registries, etc.

2. Once you find the websites that have you listed, search "remove listing from [insert website name here]." This should populate with tutorials on how to get your information removed from the specific website that has it.

   If you find sensitive information posted, such as a social security number, you can also contact the webmaster or the search engine's legal team to have it removed. For example, Google has a legal request form to report content you would like removed from Google's services. When you're getting information removed, many websites will ask for a confirmation email and/or phone number. I don't give them my main accounts. Instead, I'll create a burner email address, one that's set up under a different name and not linked to any of my personal accounts, to be used for spammy purposes. And if they ask for a phone number, again, I won't give them my actual number. I'll create a digital phone number through a service like Google Voice that will allow them to send me verification codes that I'll actually receive, but if I ever want to delete the number or change it, I can do that easily. I simply don't trust the websites not to sell the data they're collecting from me, since they're literally in the business of collecting and selling data. In general, this is a good habit to get into.

3. Create multiple online identities. This is an extension of the burner emails and digital phone numbers previously mentioned, but as a good rule of thumb, use your real information for the highly valuable websites like your bank, and for all the random stuff, use a spam email. I still check my spam email, but to minimize risk, I keep it separate from my more valuable information.

4. Set up Google Alerts for your name or social media handle. This will help you keep track of when your name pops up in news articles and on blogs or websites. Go to google.com/alerts to set up the email alerts.

5. Enlist a paid service to help keep track of your information online. There are services that focus exclusively on this, and sometimes it's offered as an extension on an antivirus package, so shop around. I haven't found any that work perfectly, but they're a good supplemental option. Before choosing a service, consider their trustworthiness, check reviews, and look into their privacy policies regarding your data.

The usual suspects

Here's a list of common people-finder websites. (This list will be most helpful for adults living in the US.) There are regulations regarding how to protect the data of minors, so it's unlikely you'll find their data on these sites, but it's still worth conducting regular searches to be sure.

- Whitepages
- BeenVerified
- Spokeo
- MyLife
- Intelius
- PeopleFinder
- FamilyTreeNow
- IMDb
- PeekYou
- PeopleFinders (the little extra *s* at the end makes all the difference)
- Advanced People Search
- US Search
- Radaris
- ThisNumber
- USA People Search
- VoterRecords
- InfoTracer
- 411Locate
- GoLookUp
- PrivateEye
- TruthFinder
- Yellow Pages
- AnyWho
- Free Background Check

Also keep in mind that data brokerage websites like these may change their names and rebrand, so there will always be more websites popping up—and that's why it's important to do these searches regularly. Aim to check monthly; think of it as part of your cleaning routine!

Be careful what you download: If it sounds too good to be true, it probably is. The app offering free money or gaming cheat codes is likely malware. Before downloading any app, check its reviews and take a look at its default settings. In some cases, it may not be worth downloading, and in other cases, you may decide to simply accept the risk because the reward is greater than the fear of a data breach. Either way, exercise caution when downloading apps onto your phone or any other device.

Antivirus software: Having a computer without antivirus software is like not locking the door to your house. Computers store our photos, work materials, and banking information, along with other important items, some of which an online burglar would be happy to stumble upon. But when we use antivirus software, it's like installing a security system in a digital house. The purpose is to protect your computer from viruses, spyware, malware, Trojans, and other cyber threats. The software scans your computer's hard drive, files, and websites visited in order to protect your data, but that doesn't mean you can ignore best practices. Antivirus software adds extra security, but it's not fool-proof. Also, be wary of companies offering free or heavily discounted antivirus software, and choose a reputable and trusted company.

Pro tip: If you're a college student, check to see if your campus offers free antivirus software.

Identity theft protection: You can monitor your identity on your own by keeping an eye on credit reports and freezing your credit, but you can also use a paid service to monitor for you, alert you of unusual activity, and help you recover hacked information, along with other add-ons. Whether you want to do it yourself or pay for the peace of mind that will come with it, identity theft is big business, so implementing a protection strategy will help you stay on top of it.

Private browsers: Private browsers, like DuckDuckGo, Vivaldi, Brave, Opera, Tor, and others help protect your data by not storing the sites you visit, cookies, usernames, and passwords. This is ideal if you share a computer at home or if you're using a public computer and want to keep your activity private. Keep in mind that using a private browser doesn't mean you're anonymous; it just means that it won't store all your data once you've closed the window. You can also adjust the settings of Safari, Firefox, or other default browsers to prevent cross-site tracking for extra privacy. And don't forget to update regularly!

Private search engines: If you're annoyed by getting a ton of ads for products just because you randomly searched for something like "lawn pillows," you'll want a private search engine. Startpage, Ecosia, and DuckDuckGo are some popular private search engines that don't track you, meaning they don't store your IP address or your search history but still deliver all the top results. In some cases, you can download browser extensions, search from the websites directly, and even use them on your phone. You can use this all the time or only when you're looking for that surprise gift. For example, when I was trying to keep my pregnancy a secret, I made sure I was using only private search engines and browsers to look up pregnancy information. Once I went public with the news, then I became a little lax, because, frankly, I wanted the ads. That said, using privacy tools covers more than whether we want innocuous ads. What else are these companies doing with the data? What *can* they do with it? The rabbit hole runs deep, so these are good habits to get into even if you don't care about ads.

Private/encrypted email services: Email is a popular entry point for hackers to gain access to data, but unless you're an enemy of the state, most people aren't worried about whether their email data is encrypted; however, there are times when even those who care little about privacy may worry. If you're sending financial documents for a new job or any kind of sensitive information via email, you open yourself up to risks if the data is breached. By using an encryption service, you make it significantly harder for a hacker to access that sensitive information. There are companies such as ProtonMail and StartMail that specialize in private email services that provide several layers of encryption. I won't get all techie, but let's just say it's super secure.

If you value your privacy, run a business with private data, are an activist, a journalist, government official, or other high-ranking security figure, using private encrypted email services should be part of your everyday routine. Also, if you hate getting ads sent to your email because you clicked on something on Facebook or Google, these providers can help with that as well.

If you're used to using a particular email service provider, it may take some time to adjust, but overall, they're easy to use, intuitive, and affordable/free, depending on the features you need.

That said, I also want to talk about a few features Gmail has, since they are the most popular email service provider. When you're composing an email, Gmail has a confidential-mode icon at the bottom of the email that, when turned on, prevents someone from forwarding, copying, printing, or downloading your email. You can also set a password on the email for added protection and set an expiration date, meaning that after that date passes, your recipient would no longer be able to view the email. It's an added step for security, but it doesn't guarantee privacy. The recipient can still take photos of the email, and if they have malicious software installed on their computer, the information could be compromised. Also, this feature doesn't replace the level of encryption some of the other services offer, but I still think it's a helpful, maybe overlooked feature.

Password managers: Our passwords are the keys to our digital life. We use them to access our emails, banking information, and social media platforms, and even though they're incredibly important, so many of us don't protect them. We use easy passwords because we need to remember them, but that makes your accounts more susceptible to hacking. You don't want your passwords to be easy; in fact, you don't even want passwords—you want long *pass phrases* with numbers and special characters. Plus, you don't want to reuse them. I know—the problem there is that you can't remember any of them. The solution? Password managers.

Today, many browsers have password managers built in, and some even monitor for leaked passwords. These are great resources because they're free and convenient, but there are a few notable differences with third-party password managers. Third-party password managers work across multiple browsers, generate passwords, and have better security, such as two-factor authentication and biometrics, to access the passwords. And being careful about what you download applies here too. This is the key to your online world, so you need to protect it, and that means going with a trusted brand.

VPNs: A virtual private network (VPN) encrypts your data to help you remain private and anonymous online. It hides your IP address, location, and identity, which is especially useful if you're connected to public Wi-Fi (i.e., at a café, hotel, school, etc.). At home, you don't necessarily need a VPN (your IP address likely changes from time to time), but in our increasingly online world, a lot of people use VPNs for extra protection. That being said, VPNs do not prevent malware or cookies on your computer from monitoring your activity, so while it's an extra layer of protection, it can't shield you if you download malicious software.

When choosing a VPN, make sure you do your research and go with a trusted and reliable VPN service, as there are some that are advertised as free but then turn out to just be scammers luring victims. So before downloading anything onto your phone or computer, whether free or a paid service, do a little digging and make sure it's a reputable brand. I'm personally more comfortable with the paid services like Nord, Express, and Proton. Some antivirus software packages even come with VPNs, so if you're shopping for a bunch of services, you may be able to package them all; but always check out the reviews before deciding.

Hotspots: Hotspots are usually used by business travelers who need a fast and secure internet connection. Companies often provide hotspots because they don't want an employee to accidentally compromise their internal data by connecting to vulnerable public Wi-Fi. The average person may not need a hotspot unless they travel a lot or don't want to eat up their data allotment using their phone's mobile hotspot feature, but if you're working with sensitive data while on the go, a hotspot is necessary. You can use it to connect with your laptop, phone, gaming console, smart TV, etc.

EXIF data/metadata: A picture is worth a thousand words, and if someone is looking at a photo's metadata, it could reveal more than we'd like. When we snap a picture from our phone or a camera, the image is embedded with details about the photo known as EXIF data, or metadata. This information could include the camera model, aspect ratio, and other details about the photo, such as the location where the photo was taken (depending on camera settings). Unless you're a photographer, you've probably never looked at a photo's metadata, but there are times when it's worth thinking about.

Let's say you're selling something online. Depending on your camera's settings, that photo could include the coordinates of where that photo was taken. If it's a vacation photo, maybe it's not a big deal, but if it's a photo you took in your house, you might think twice before basically sending a stranger your address. The good news is there's a very easy nontechie way to remove metadata—simply take a screenshot! That's it. When you take a screenshot, you remove the metadata, so then you can send your screenshot via text or email versus the original photo. It's an extra step, but it's so easy you'll hardly notice.

And the news gets better. If you're posting photos on social media like Instagram, Facebook, Tumblr, and more, most of these well-known apps delete or hide the location-specific data so it can't be tracked. This applies to anything you post or send via direct messages. So, for most of your day-to-day activities, you won't have to worry about data on your photos. The only times it's come up for me are when I'm loading photos to a website I don't trust (like an interior design website) and when I'm selling something. Also, if you're posting on blogs, forums, or apps and aren't sure about their security, you might want to try the screenshot method.

The Parler app is a good example of when metadata and security matter. In 2021, a lone hacker discovered security vulnerabilities within the Parler app and began scraping data from the site. After recruiting help from others, the team had obtained millions of posts, videos, and photos that included user location data, because unlike Instagram and Facebook, Parler hadn't removed that information. In 2020, I remember seeing TikTok pranks where people were posting sexy photos to Parler and dropping their Venmo or Cash App handle. When I'd see these videos, I'd remind those posters to remove the metadata, and about three months later, the site was breached. No matter the intentions of the hackers or hacktivists, when they scrape or breach, it's universal. They're working with massive data sets and aren't accounting for everyone's intent when joining a platform, so it's up to you to help mitigate the risks whenever possible.

The average person may not be scraping hacker forums and databases just to find an address, but there are companies that do that. Once records are public, there are companies that compile this information, and that's one of the ways it can end up on people-search websites. Unlike dark net hacker forums, people-search websites are very easy to use and accessible to anyone who can manage a search engine results page.

In short, while metadata may seem techie, there are a couple of situations when you should care: first, when you are texting or emailing photos to a stranger; and second, when you're uploading photos to a website or app that isn't secure. If you're doing one of those things, screenshot your photo to protect the data.

Also, I had mentioned that the location data is based on phone or camera settings. You can disable the location-tagging feature on cameras and phones, but I personally leave it on. I do that because I have about twenty thousand photos in my camera roll, so if I'm looking for a photo I know I took in Miami, I like having the ability to search "Miami" and have all my photos come up.

HOW TO AVOID GETTING HACKED
OR HAVING YOUR DATA LEAKED

Is there a guaranteed way to never get hacked or experience a data breach? No; chances are, you'll experience a breach at some point, if you haven't already. But are there best practices to help you avoid falling victim to a cyber threat? Yes—and here's a list of my top tips.

✓ **Question more.** Trust less. This rule applies to nearly everything online. Just because a product has five stars doesn't mean it's not a scam. Did you read the reviews? Do they look like they were written by people or bots? The ad on your favorite social media page could be paid for by a scammer the same way a real company can pay for one. If something seems unusual or too good to be true, question it, because it probably is.

✓ **Always update your operating system, apps, and software.** These updates often include security updates.

✓ **Avoid unusual links.** We get these via email, text, and direct messages. We try to avoid the obvious ones, but one giveaway is if the link is asking you to take action, like providing log-in information with your password. If you click on a link that unexpectedly asks you to take action, then that's a moment to take a pause and verify the validity of the link before providing any additional information. There are many ways to verify if a link is valid, but a quick one is to use a search engine and look at the time stamp of the message you received. If it's a known scam, you'll see lots of people talking about it online.

✓ **Cross-check the link.** It's always best to avoid clicking on suspicious links, but if you can't figure out if the link is real or not, copy and paste the URL into VirusTotal.com. This site will analyze suspicious files and URLs to detect any malware, and it shares the information with the security community. It's not a foolproof method, but it's helpful. Also remember that, because it shares information, you shouldn't upload anything private.

✓ **If you get a suspicious email, check the sender's address before taking any action.** A lot of scams will say they're from your bank or a government office, but then when you look at the address, it's from a Gmail or Yahoo account. That's a dead giveaway that something is a scam.

✓ **Use multifactor authentication,** preferably with authenticator apps instead of text-based authentication whenever possible.

✓ **Use long pass phrases** instead of passwords.

✓ **Back up your data and always have an off-line backup** like an external hard drive.

✓ **Don't post information that can help someone access your online accounts.** This can include pet names, birthdays, the city where you grew up, etc.

✓ **Setting up your password-recovery questions? Lie.** Only you should know the answers to those questions, so if multiple people know the breed of your first dog and that's a security question, then make something up.

✓ **When downloading an app, don't settle for the default settings.** Take a look at what those settings are and adjust them to be what's actually necessary to run the app.

✓ **Invest in cybersecurity technologies** like password managers and antivirus software.

✓ **Avoid automatically saving your passwords in your browsers and apps,** particularly the log-in information for sensitive accounts such as your loans, emails, social media profiles, and school information. If a hacker gets into your computer, autofill log-ins can quickly give them access to a lot of personal information. I know this can be inconvenient, but that's where a password manager with multistep protection can help.

✓ **Create email accounts specifically for sensitive information** and others for mass emails, like those from news sources or promo emails from retailers.

✓ **When possible, use a burner number** from a service such as Google Voice when signing up for things online or for in-store promotions when you don't really want or need to give out your phone number.

✓ **If budget allows, consider a PO box.** This is particularly important if you freelance or have a side hustle where you're frequently giving out your address to strangers.

✓ **When shopping, consider moving over to a digital wallet** such as Apple Pay, which provides more security features than your credit card, such as two-factor authentication or facial recognition. The same applies when shopping online. Using a platform like PayPal, which offers end-to-end encryption, is safer than inputting your credit card information directly into a merchant's site. When we shop online, we use so many websites that it's hard to keep track of who has what if/when a company gets hacked. On the other hand, with PayPal (or a similar service), everything is encrypted and in one place. Not even the merchants get your credit card information—they only get your username and other personal information. The only downside is if you're returning something in the store, they might not be able to look up your purchase with your card, so you'll need the receipt or to opt for store credit.

✓ **Get credit card offers at home? Shred them.** Shred anything with personal information before throwing it into the trash (or use an identity theft protection stamp). Your bills, bank records, labels on prescription bottles, college letters, anything with a signature on it—shred it all! And if you don't have a shredder at home or have too much to shred, look up local document-shredding events. They're often held at community centers.

✓ **Sign up for scam alerts with the Better Business Bureau.** They regularly track and report on common scams and send you email updates on what those scams are.

HOW TO KNOW IF YOUR DATA HAS BEEN BREACHED

A data breach is when confidential or protected information is accessed, stolen, and used by a cybercriminal without authorization. Usually a company, school, or app gets hacked, and whatever information is collected could be used maliciously. The information could include passwords, your social security number, phone number, emails, and a ton of other stuff you wouldn't want floating around.

When there's a data breach, a company is legally required to notify users. Often it's done via email, but sometimes their announcements are delayed or hidden in public statements, or maybe you've changed your email, so unless you're following the news, you may not even know you've been compromised.

Here are a few easy ways to check whether your data has been compromised:

- **HaveIBeenPwned.com:** This is a database that can check whether your email, phone number, or passwords have been leaked. It's a free service maintained by security experts, and if your data hasn't been leaked, you can set up notifications on the site so you'll know if and when it happens in the future.

- **Password managers:** Whether you're using a password manager built into your web browser or a more versatile service, a password manager will run checks on your accounts and let you know if anything has been compromised.

- **Dark web monitoring:** If you've purchased an antivirus software plan, it likely comes with other features such as dark web monitoring, which scans the dark web for your personal data. In the plan I have, I can upload insurance information, emails, credit cards, and even gamer tags for my service to monitor; if there's a breach and my service finds it, they'll notify me. If you have an identity theft protection service, that can monitor even more of your personal data (depending on the plan you select).

WHAT ABOUT SCAMS?

There are different types of scams, but ultimately, a scam tricks you in order to take money and/or personal information from you. It could be a phishing scam, which deceives you into giving away information like a bank log-in, it could be a fake ad on Facebook that tricks you into buying a counterfeit product (assuming you ever receive it), and of course, there are the in-person scams (more on this in the travel section).

Scams can reach us via email, text, direct messages, comments on our social media pages, gaming chat rooms, and ever-annoying phone calls. We're fortunate that when we're online, many email services and browsers will warn us of suspicious links, but when we're on the phone or in an app, it may be harder to see the warning signs.

Here are a few ways to avoid getting caught up in a scam
- If it seems too good to be true, it probably is.

- In your smartphone settings, you can send all incoming unknown callers directly to voice mail. If it's important, someone will leave a message or text you, or you can disable this feature when you're expecting a lot of unknown calls, like when applying for a job.

- If you receive an incoming call, text, or email asking you for personal information, your warning signals should start blaring. It could be someone pretending to be someone you know, your bank, tech support, or the government. If it sounds legitimate but you're still not sure, the best way to handle it is to hang up and call the official number (do not call back the number that called you). Also make sure you type in the number correctly, because if you mistype it, that could lead to another type of scam.

- Pay attention to the URL you're being directed or redirected to before clicking on it.

- If you get a pop-up on your computer or phone warning you of a technical problem, exit out.

- Scams usually have a sense of urgency attached. "Claim your prize today!" "Your account is suspended!" "Your purchase didn't go through!" These are all tricks to get you to act quickly so you spend less time investigating whether it's real or not.

- A scam will ask you to take an action—to sign in, provide a PIN, or enter your password. If you receive an email or text out of nowhere with a link that redirects you to a log-in page or that asks you to send information right away, it's probably a scam, even if it looks real.

- Before clicking on a link or a button, right click (or hover), copy the URL, and paste it into a Word document or note. This will show you the full link so you can see exactly what kind of website you're visiting. You can also paste any suspicious links into a website like VirusTotal.com to see if it contains malware. It's best to avoid clicking on the links to begin with, but if you're not sure, try the above.

- Watch for bad grammar and typos. So many scam ads, emails, and texts have a ton of grammar mistakes and are simply poorly written, but when we're spending hours scrolling through our feeds or emails, we might miss these important clues. Take your time.

- When browsing online, watch out for fake ads and classifieds. Again, if it sounds too good to be true, it is. The $5,000 purse is not on sale, brand-new, for only $65. It's counterfeit, or worse—the ad is an attempt to steal your money.

- If you're being asked to pay online via money order, wire transfer, mailed gift cards, or in a peer-to-peer payment app, remember that these purchases aren't protected. It's like handing over cash.

- If you want to know if a company is real, look it up. You can type it into Google or your preferred search engine with the keyword *scam* to read what others are saying, and you can look up the company on Trustpilot.com.

- When you see an ad on a social media profile, look at the comments. I've seen several that are obvious bots commenting on the ad to make it seem legitimate. Some giveaways are when the comments are all similar in that they're positive and make the same kinds of grammatical mistakes. Even worse, sometimes you'll see ads that say there are hundreds of comments on the post, but when you click on it there are no comments. This is because the scammer disabled them. Legitimate companies don't do that.

- Speaking of social media, don't add friends that you don't know on a private account, and remember: scams can still come through your direct messages or from your friends and family's accounts if they've been hacked or phished.

- Look out for comments in chat rooms or on social media pages promising a great investment, crypto, or anything else that, again, sounds too good to be true. This includes spammy romance comments.

- If you come across a post or message online that seems suspicious, investigate the profile. Often, you'll find that scammers will create a profile and offer something that seems too good to be true, like a great job posting or cute puppies for adoption. These are red flags.

- Scammers can pose as legitimate businesses but will change one letter or add a phrase like "official account" to trick you. Look at the profile photo, check the grammar, and take the time to type the company's name into a search engine and see what their official social media pages are. These are steps that may take a few minutes but can save you a lot in the long run. And remember, scammers can also pose as your family and friends. If you see a post of theirs or get a message from them saying that they need you to send them money via Cash App, they've likely been hacked. Take a moment to call them or contact them in another way to confirm whether the message is real. If we all took an extra minute to become mini FBI agents, scammers would have to work a lot harder to take advantage of us.

YOU'VE IDENTIFIED A SCAM—NOW WHAT?

The first thing is don't respond. I know it's fun to see the viral videos of people messing with scammers, but all you're doing is confirming that your email and phone number are valid, which means you can get more spam. Ignore the message.

Next, you can report the email, post, or text as spam. On social media, you can report both the spam comments and the account that posted it. If enough people report it, the platform might just remove the account. With email, you can report it right in the platform, and with text messages, you may be able to report them directly within your phone. Some phones don't have that functionality, so you can forward the message to 7726. (This works in the US, Canada, and the UK.) This helps your service provider and security providers prevent spam. When you forward spam to 7726, your service provider will reply by asking you for the phone number that sent the spam message; reply back with the phone number, and that's it. You've done your good deed for the day!

Finally, block it. Whether you got a spam call, email, text, or even a direct message on social media, block the sender. It's worth noting that many cell phone providers offer free apps to help filter spam messages. Within these apps you can report spam, adjust what kind of spam gets automatically blocked, and add numbers to your blocked list. I'm a big fan of these apps; on my phone they block hundreds of annoying spam calls.

If you want to be a superhero, there's one more step you can take. Report the scam to the Federal Trade Commission at reportfraud.ftc.gov. You can report annoying calls, fake health ads, lottery scams, impersonators, and bad business practices. It takes a little longer than simply blocking or forwarding a message, but it helps the FTC identify trends so they can educate and protect other people. You can also report fraud on the phone by calling 1-877-FTC-HELP (382-4357).

Additionally, visit donotcall.gov. You can register your home and mobile phones on the National Do Not Call Registry for free. It prevents telemarketers from calling you, although you'll still get calls from other organizations such as charities or political groups. If you do get a call from a telemarketer, you can report the unwanted call on this website as well. This may not stop the scammers—they generally don't care about rules or registries—but it can reduce other unwanted calls.

COMMON SCAMS TO LOOK OUT FOR

We've talked about some of the ways to avoid getting swindled, but one of the fastest ways is to be able to quickly recognize a scam for what it is. I know that if I get a call from the "Social Security Administration," it's 100 percent a scam, and I immediately hang up. That type of government agency would never cold-call directly. The officialness of the name is used as a lure—don't fall for it.

Getting familiar with common scams will help you identify them quickly too, so you can shut them down fast. Even though scams are constantly changing, they tend to keep to a lot of the same traits that we've discussed: they're too good to be true, there's a sense of urgency, and they're asking you to take action.

Here's a look at some of the common scams you're likely to come across:

Phishing Scams: These are likely the most common type of scam you'll come across. They involve a cybercriminal trying to get you to hand over information, often by using spoofed links or websites. Phishing attempts can come via text message, social media messages or posts, gaming chat rooms, email, and even voice mail. The valuable information they seek can include passwords, bank details like your credit card numbers, social security numbers, and more, which can be used to make fraudulent purchases, steal identities, or hack social media accounts.

The consequences of falling for a phishing scam can be horrific, but if you quickly recognize phishing attempts, you're much less likely to fall for them. Let's review a few common scenarios:

- You've won a prize and need to claim it right away!

- We're confirming your order of our very expensive product (sent from a company you've never heard of or done business with).

- You have to update your payment method ASAP.

- Your account is being deactivated.

- Your credit card has been compromised.

- Your account has been hacked or threatened; click here to verify your profile.

- You qualify for verification on Instagram—just fill out this form!

- We've updated our policy. Please confirm your account.

- Hey, it's tech support and we need you to install new software.

- You've violated our copyright policy and will be in trouble unless you dispute it.

- I'm your boss and I need you to do me a favor, buy gift cards, or transfer money.

- I'm your boss and a customer complained. This is very urgent and you must open the attachment!

- I made this for you.

- OMG, you're on the ugly list at school!

- Track your package.

- Oops, I accidentally sent you money. (Often on Venmo or Cash App.)

These are all examples of common phishing scams you're likely to encounter. They're often followed up by a link or attachment that you need to click on. It could look real, or maybe it's just a combination of random letters and numbers, or maybe it's a Google form or a button, but in most cases you'll be asked to click, open, or download something, and do so fast.

In each of these situations the cybercriminal is trying to get you to act urgently. If the message comes from an unknown number or weird email, you might catch on quickly, but what if it comes from your mom or your best friend via WhatsApp or Instagram? Remember that these messages can come from anywhere, and they can look real. This is the time to call upon your years of experience searching for Waldo as a kid, except this time you're looking for criminal red flags.

So how do you find Waldo in these phishing attacks, and how do you avoid getting caught up in them? There are a few best practices that you should implement 24-7, whether you're at work, gaming, browsing your social media feed, or chatting.

1. **Trust less, no matter who it is!** Cybercriminals know you're more likely to trust a WhatsApp message from your mom telling you she forgot the Amazon login or your boss telling you that you're in trouble. Remember that everyone can get phished this way, so when our friends, colleagues, or family members get hacked, we're at risk as well. No matter who's sending the message, if there's a link or attachment, proceed with caution.

2. Look for a sense of urgency. Most of the time a scammer wants you to act quickly; they might try to scare you or get you excited—whatever it takes to make sure you quickly do what they need you to do. If someone is trying to get you to do something fast, it's a red flag!

3. Look for the action. Cybercriminals need you to hand over your information, which they usually do by asking you to open an attachment, download something, or click on a link. In most cases, they'll ask you to do it ASAP. If a message seems urgent and is asking you to take action, you should already be heading to the report, block, and delete buttons.

4. Check the grammar. Oftentimes when you spot weird grammar mistakes, you might think, *Wow, that was lazy. The scammer put all this effort into trying to scam me and I can barely understand it.* In some cases you'd be right: the translation was bad, and they were too lazy to fix it. In other cases, however, the poor grammar is intentional. In marketing, this might be referred to as a lead qualifier. Essentially, if someone is acting so quickly that they don't notice the little mistakes, it means they're more likely to act quickly in handing over their private information. This makes the scammer's job easier. And, ultimately, it's a numbers game, meaning that they don't need millions of people to fall for it—they just need one.

5. Check the sender. Who's sending you this very important message that's asking you to act? Do you recognize the phone number, email, or social media account? Are you sure? Is the profile verified? Is the email spelled correctly? Is it an official email or is it coming from a Gmail or Yahoo account? Think about these questions before taking any further action.

6. **Hover over links.** Let's say all of the above checks out and you're starting to think it's a legitimate message—but you're not done! Next, check the link. In an email you can hover your cursor over the link or right-click it to see if it contains anything unusual. A link might say Amazon but when you hover over it you notice it's actually www.amason.net/Aso9f7szbfnl. If you're on your phone, you can press and hold on the link, and you'll see the option to copy it. Paste the link into a notes document to see if it's legit, or head to VirusTotal.com to find out whether anyone else has reported the link as being malicious. Always investigate before you click, and if you can avoid clicking, that's your best bet.

7. **Check attachment extensions.** If a message wants you to open an attachment, is it a standard .jpg, .png, .pdf, .wav, .mp4 or .mp3? These are file formats you've probably interacted with before, and they're generally safe to open, unless the cybercriminal has disguised their attachment as something safe. If a file is a .zip or .rar, proceed with caution. Before opening it, you might want to head to VirusTotal.com and upload the file to see if it contains anything malicious. Be sure to not upload anything private. Also, if you see any duplicated file extensions like MyDocument.jpg.exe, don't open it—it's likely a virus.

8. **Confirm with the sender.** Depending on who sends you the message, try to call them to make sure it's real. If the caller is in fact someone you know and trust, any confusion can be cleared up quickly. Remember not to call any phone numbers that are provided in the email. If the hacker is smart, they'll foresee that and change the number. You can always go to your search engine and

look up an official number; ideally, you should do this
before doing the previous two steps.

9. **Enable two-factor (2FA) or multifactor
   authentication.** I know I'm repeating myself here,
   but it's important. I strongly suggest that you enable
   2FA on as many accounts as possible. Enabling 2FA
   means that anytime you want to log into your account or
   even make a purchase, you'll have to provide a special
   code. If a scammer gets your password and you have
   2FA enabled, they still won't have enough information to
   get into your account. This gives you the time you need
   to quickly change your password and hope they move
   on to another target. Keep in mind that it's possible for
   a hacker to bypass this extra security measure if you
   provide them with the code or if they have your phone.
   If anyone ever texts you saying they're going to send
   you a code, they're more than likely trying to reset the
   password on one of your accounts—don't give it to
   them.

10. **Oops, I got phished.** This is the worst-case
    scenario, but there's still hope. Make immediate moves
    to change your password, cancel your card, put a freeze
    on your credit—essentially, do whatever you can to
    preempt the damage. (This is one of the reasons that
    it's important not to reuse passwords, because if you
    do fall for a phishing attack and hand over password
    information, it's a lot easier to change one password
    quickly than it is to change twenty.)

That's a brief overview of phishing, but I don't want to mislead you
into thinking that the above are foolproof methods. In most cases
they're enough. A scammer has a job to do, and there's no reason for

them to stick with someone who's making their job more difficult when there are so many easier targets. That said, if they're skilled and if they want to, they'll try to figure out a way to obtain your information. But in most cases, they'll just move on if you avoid the suspicious links and attachments.

Unfortunately, we're not done. There are still so many scams you might come across that may or may not involve phishing, so on we go to the next.

Investment scams: If you're approached to invest via social media, it's likely a scam. I see five to ten of these per day. They're pervasive, promise high returns with low risk, and in the end, you lose your money. They often reference cryptocurrency as well.

To avoid this scam, do your research and opt for trusted investment sources. Do not let strangers on the internet pressure you into accepting their deals, and don't trust their unsolicited offers.

Relationship scams: These are vicious, and they come in different forms. The romance scams traditionally start online—you're told the person loves you and perhaps wants to marry you, but they've fallen on hard times and need your help. This "help" usually involves money that you'll never see again. Maybe they're working on an oil rig, are in the military, or are a doctor working with an international organization, but then they have trouble with customs or need to pay for travel documents to get home. Again, it's a lie, and any money that's wired or loaded onto a card is stolen. Another version is getting a call that your loved one is in trouble—usually that they've had an accident or have been arrested. The person on the phone tells you they need cash urgently to get them out of trouble. This is another common scam.

To avoid this scam, trust less. Unless you've met in person, you never know who's on the other side of online profiles. You can try investigating a bit by looking at the activity of the account, checking social media profiles, reverse-searching photos they may send you, or looking up the scenario online to see if people are discussing it as a common scam. These are tough, because when the heart is involved, reason can take a back seat. But try to take a step back and evaluate the situation, especially if you're being asked for money.

Employment scams: When looking for work, you'll likely come across jobs offering great pay working from home with no experience. They often target college students and entry-level workers. They may even go as far as having you interview for the job, which you "get" right away. Once you accept the job, you're asked to purchase supplies from a website and told that you'll be reimbursed for the cost. This is likely a scam, and you will not be reimbursed.

To avoid this scam, never send a prospective employer money as part of accepting a job. Also, look up the company and the job listing, and you can even go as far as calling the company to verify that the job listing is legitimate. Another red flag is if the person interviewing you won't turn on their camera.

Housing scams: These scams often feature a deal that's too good to be true because it is. Usually, the photos are gorgeous, the price is well below average, there isn't a screening process, and it's available right away. Often the landlord lives abroad as well, so they need you to wire money in order to receive the keys.

To avoid these scams, always see the unit in person, meet the listing agent in person or via a video walk-through, always sign a lease, and avoid handing over money before you have any of the details settled. Also, you can look up reviews and reverse-search the images to see if they're being reused from another legitimate listing.

Charity scams: Some scammers set up fake charities in order to try to take advantage of people, particularly if there's been a natural disaster or some kind of tragedy. Sometimes they use names that sound similar to a charity you probably already know.

To avoid this scam, look up a charity online. There are a variety of websites that rate charities based on their transparency, and you can even check their Better Business Bureau ratings. On the phone, you can confirm the exact name, website, and mailing address of a charity.

Government grant scams: These scammers will call with great news! The government is going to give you a grant for college or to repair your roof, and all you have to do is pay a one-time fee or give them your bank information so they can deposit the money into your account. SCAM! Grants have extensive application processes and usually go toward organizations or government agencies or schools that are working on research projects that benefit the public. The government is not replacing your roof randomly.

To avoid this scam, be wary of anyone who calls you saying they're from the government. Also, don't assume the name on your caller ID is actually who's calling, as scammers can disguise their real phone numbers and locations to make it look like they're calling from somewhere else. And don't pay any fees or provide bank account information to anyone who calls you about a grant you've "won." If you're interested in how grants work, you can learn more at grants.gov.

Prize scams: Another "Wow—what great news!" scam. You've won the lottery, a contest, or a sweepstakes, and all you have to do is pay a fee to collect it. Nope.

To avoid this scam, ask yourself, *Did I enter any contests?* If you didn't, hang up. If you did, ask them to confirm the name of the organization. Do not pay any fees or taxes or wire any money in order to claim your prize, and do not provide any banking information simply because the person on the phone is pressuring you to.

Online shopping scams: These come in a variety of ways. It could be a Google ad or something you see on Facebook Marketplace or for sale on Reddit (or any selling app). These scam ads are technically not allowed, and when they're caught, Google and Facebook remove them, but with millions of ads out there, it's unlikely the tech giants can catch them all.

Generally, the way these scams get your interest is by advertising a high-value item for a fraction of its retail cost. A $600 vacuum listed for only $75 brand-new, in the box, and shipped right to your door doesn't make any sense. Even if you did receive a vacuum, it would probably be a knockoff, but often you never receive the item.

When you message the person regarding this "too good to be true" deal, they will typically tell you their payment option in the app isn't working and that they'll need you to send the money through a peer-to-peer money-transfer app like Venmo or PayPal. The problem here is that if you're sending money the way you would send money to a friend, it's not protected. You could lose it, and there's no way the apps can help you get it back.

Another version of this online shopping scam is when you see an ad for your favorite pair of shoes. When you click on the ad, you may notice the URL isn't the company's regular website. You might get a completely different item in the mail, or you might get your credit card information stolen.

You may also see these scams when you're selling something on a public marketplace for used goods. Someone might message you saying they're very interested and can pick up the item right away but would rather communicate via text message instead. Then suddenly they say they're going to text you a verification code because they want to confirm you're a real person. What a smart, high-tech buyer, right? Wrong. They're a scammer, and when you give them that code, they're going to hack whatever account you just gave them access to by texting them that code. Once the hacker gets into your account, they will reset the password and all the identifying features associated with the account so you can't get it back. In some cases, they might ask you to pay them in order to get your account back, but in other cases, it's more valuable for them to keep the account.

There are other iterations of this scam as well, but the general theme is that if it sounds too good to be true, it is.

To avoid this scam, follow the too-good-to-be-true rule. Also, don't allow people to move conversations off the app where you're selling items. Sometimes it's inconvenient because texts to your phone are much easier to see than messages in an app, but if you're selling something, simply check your app more often. The moment someone tries to take the conversation off the app, that should raise a red flag.

Also try to keep your number private, and don't give it to strangers. If you feel you need to give a number to a potential buyer for convenience, try a burner number instead, such as a Google Voice number. And lastly, if anyone asks you for a verification code of any sort that's being texted to your phone, do not provide it. These codes are meant to be private and are not to be shared with anyone under any circumstances. The only time you should use these codes is when you're trying to make purchases or changing information on your own accounts. You shouldn't be giving them to strangers.

Financial app scams: There are a few ways to get scammed via financial apps. I've already mentioned one above, but I want to bring your attention to a few more. A scammer might pretend to be your friend and request money from you through an app; they might say you've won an award or that you need to pay for tech support service via Venmo, Cash App, PayPal, or Zelle; they might call and pretend to be a representative of the app, asking for a "verification code." (That's a huge red flag, as these apps won't call you—plus, you should never share a verification code.) They might even mail you a paper check and ask you to pay them back via the app. Some scams are easier to spot than others, but the one that I think is trickiest to spot is when someone "accidentally" sends you money and then messages you with something like, "Hey, I sent that money to the wrong account, would you mind sending it back?" You sympathize, because we all make mistakes, and maybe you're tempted to send the money back, but don't. It's likely that the scammer has used a stolen bank account to send you money, and when the theft is reported, that money will be taken out of your account. In the meantime, if you send the scammer money, you'll be sending it to their personal account, and since peer-to-peer transactions aren't protected, the money will be gone.

Separately, if you ever lend your phone to someone, make sure you've logged out of these apps. Someone could pretend their phone battery died and ask to borrow your phone, then send themselves money from your app. Protect any financial apps you may have on your phone or any other device by not saving login information and using extra layers of security, like facial recognition, when available.

ONLINE GAMING

There are billions of gamers, both adults and children, who love to play on their mobile devices, consoles, and computers alike, but the popularity of online gaming also draws the attention of some bad actors. Scam artists use gaming chats to trick people into giving up financial information, downloading malware, or paying for gaming enhancements that don't exist. Here are a few ways to protect ourselves when gaming online:

- **Don't reuse passwords:** And we're back to the basics! But it's true for all your accounts: reusing passwords is a risk, and that applies to gaming accounts as well. Scammers can get password and username information that's been stolen or leaked from the dark web or use automated software to hack into accounts. They may not get a ton of accounts this way, but even a few are enough to access personal information and make fraudulent credit card purchases. As with all online accounts, don't reuse passwords, and use long, strong passwords (or pass phrases).

- **Check your settings:** This also applies to all the apps we have installed on our phones, televisions, computers, and more. Check your security settings to opt out of having your data sold, enable two-factor or multifactor authentication, set up account notifications, and enable any parental controls such as blocking in-app purchases or limiting the servers the account can play on. With some apps, you can even filter out comments that have certain words, which you can use to filter out bullying and common scam language to limit unwanted social interaction.

- **Be careful what you download:** One way scammers gain access to accounts is by tricking people into downloading malware. They'll make their app or game seem legitimate and, in doing so, infect devices with malicious code or viruses. Depending on the hacker's intent, their code can spy on private messages, log your keystrokes, and even take control of your device remotely. To avoid this, only download games from well-known gaming platforms and do your research before downloading from websites you're not familiar with. For parents, I'd recommend enabling the requirement of a password for any downloads and instructing your kids that downloads of any sort are not permitted without parental permission.

- **Get familiar with common scams:** If you know what's coming, you can easily avoid it. Some of the most common scams involve cheat codes, upgrades, and free game bucks in exchange for a trade or financial information. Scammers will spam message boards and online chats saying they have these game enhancements, but they have no intention of delivering. Gamers may trade or pay for the upgrades or boosts, usually with a peer-to-peer payment app, but the money will get stolen and you won't get the game upgrades. To avoid this, never buy game enhancements from someone you don't know or have only "met" online. Only purchase game upgrades directly from the developer.

Phishing attempts are another common scam targeting gamers. They can come in the form of a text or email threatening to close your gaming account unless you update your financial information. When you get a message like this, you can always look it up online to see what other people are reporting. Many apps will only ask for sensitive information in the app and won't send you links to provide that information. Still, if you're unsure, you can look it up online and follow the other steps outlined in the phishing section of this book.

- **Use antivirus software:** Antivirus and malware protection software are traditionally thought of as being exclusive to computers, but with the popularity of online gaming and our mobile devices, companies have now developed antivirus software for our mobile devices. If you already have antivirus software, you may have this feature and not even realize it. Some companies even have specific plans that are limited to gaming only, so if you want to take that extra step to protect your devices, investing in security software may be the way to go.

- **Talk to your kids:** If you have children who game online, help them identify and learn how to deal with online risks. Warn them about the public gaming chats and teach them to report any bullying or uncomfortable conversations right away, not to share personal information, to use an anonymous handle and avatar, and to avoid illegal downloads. Teach your kids about some of the common questions they may come across in gaming chats and how not to share their age, school, or city, or agree to meet in person anyone they've met online. Tell them how other gamers might lie about who they are and pretend to be kids when they're adults. Let them know about some of the common scams and how they might be tricked into a false trade. Overall, empower them to protect themselves, and keep these conversations going all the time. It's not a one-off conversation but a constant and open dialogue.

PREDATORS AND SEXTORTION

Predators and their intended victims come in all shapes and sizes, but when we're talking about online gaming, the victims are often children and teens. Growing up with technology, children are comfortable sharing information about themselves online, and predators know how to manipulate that. It's become such a problem that in 2019, the Federal Bureau of Investigation launched a sextortion awareness campaign in schools, teaching children about the risks, the signs, and how to report these predatory crimes.[1] Criminals might offer gifts and money or threaten a child to produce an explicit image or video. The predator will then use these images to threaten harm or exposure if the child stops producing content.

To avoid this, it's important to have open, educational conversations about online risks. Teach children to avoid moving conversations to another app if they've met someone online, and remind them that any image or video sent to this stranger can be made public.

If your child has a public persona, you may want to show them examples of appropriate and inappropriate interactions. But regardless of whether your child has a public persona, you should monitor their online interactions. It can be an activity that you and your child do together, so it feels like a collaborative effort where you praise them for what they've done correctly and give them the opportunity to learn from and correct any mistakes. Also, if any of your children's friends are going through one of the aforementioned situations, let your child know that they can count on you for help. It can be hard for children to navigate whether they'll get in trouble if they ask for help, so without going into all of the behavioral theories, let's just say this will be an ongoing parental experiment.

CHAPTER 4

MOM FRIEND ON THE GO: SAFETY AND CONVENIENCE AWAY FROM HOME

To me, the two most iconic symbols of a Mom Friend are jam-packed purses and cars. Because whatever doesn't fit in the purse is definitely stashed somewhere in the car. My car has a change of clothes, flip-flops in case I get caught in a storm or decide to get a last-minute pedi, an elaborate first aid kit, a pet first aid kit that also includes food, leashes, and towels in case I come across an animal in need, a sweater (of course), flashlights, glow sticks, paper towels, a bottle of water (which I rotate), duct tape, cleaning cloths . . . I could go on. In my car's center console, I even used to keep a travel-size flat iron and a full makeup kit. The more I write this, the more I realize I'm exposing myself, but it's a trait I'm proud of and one people appreciate when they're in need.

When a friend ripped his pants, guess who had a sewing kit and sewed those bad boys right up? When my girls and I hosted an impromptu beach BBQ, guess whose car had emergency cups, napkins, and a tool that could be used to baste chicken for the grill? And after a night of clubbing when everyone else was on the verge of throwing up, guess who had double-bagged baggies, water, and paper towels already prepped for the ride home? It may seem like overkill, but in those moments, we were comfortable because one girl (me) was the ultimate Mom Friend of the group.

Here's a closer look at safety and convenience items you can keep in or on your car, many of which I use:

A jump starter: An absolute must! This is by far my favorite and most-used item in my car. Over time, jump starters have become so compact they're lightweight and can even fit in a purse. My jump starter can jump-start a car, SUV, and even a boat if needed, but it fits in the palm of my hand. It also has a built-in flashlight and USB ports so I can charge my phone or other electronics. The charging function is what I use it for the most. I prefer it to charging with my car's USB port because it's faster. I also always take it with me when I travel abroad because hotels usually have limited outlets, and particularly when I'm traveling in places with different electrical voltages, my devices typically have to compete over which gets charged first. Will it be the phone, the camera, the iPad, or the laptop? With my portable charger, I can charge more devices at once even when on long train, plane, or bus rides. If you had to choose only one item to keep in your car, I'd 100 percent recommend a jump starter.

Flat-tire repair kit: Even though I have a roadside assistance service, I still like to keep a flat-tire repair kit in my car. A flat tire is inconvenient and dangerous, but for twenty or thirty dollars, you can get a kit that includes an aerosol pressurized sealant, which will buy you a few extra miles so you can get your car serviced without having to wait for someone to come to you. They work best on small punctures and when accompanied by an air compressor so you can inflate your car tire.

Glow sticks / flashlights: I was in college driving to a late-night movie when my tire blew out on the road. It was scary to feel like I had lost control of the car; plus, I was alone on a dark highway. My fear was that a distracted driver might plow into me while I was waiting for service, so I set up glow sticks along with using my hazard lights to help other drivers take notice of my car and to help roadside assistance find me. Glow sticks are ideal because they can be used in the rain, they last a long time in your car, anyone can operate them, they're nonflammable, and they're inexpensive. You can use flashlights as well, but depending on the type of light, it may not be able to get wet; plus, you might need the flashlight for other things. For example, if you're servicing your car, you might need the flashlight to be able to see what you're doing while the glow sticks outline your car so other drivers know it's disabled. I've also purchased flashing glow sticks at a dollar store for this purpose.

Antitheft screws: Believe it or not, people steal license plates. It could be that the thief is driving a stolen car, has a suspended license, or maybe they don't have insurance—whatever the reason, having your plates stolen is a pain. In 2021, this happened to my mom. She filed a police report, had to replace the plates, and was told she couldn't drive her car until the new plates arrived. Definitely inconvenient! If you're parking your car in public, whether it's your driveway, street parking, mall parking, or any parking lot, consider getting antitheft screws.

Normally, thieves looking to steal license plates have a screwdriver on them, but antitheft screws have a proprietary head that won't work with your standard screwdriver. Hopefully that's enough to make a thief move on to an easier target. Antitheft screws are only a few dollars, so they're a small investment. Also, make sure you know your license plate number in case it is stolen—it'll be easier for you to report it. You can save a photo of it on your phone or check your vehicle registration. If you've used an app to park your car, it might have that information saved, so there are a few ways to access it in a pinch.

Along similar lines, depending on your state, thieves can steal the renewal sticker on your license plate. Some states have precut the stickers so they don't tear off in one piece, 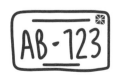 making it harder for thieves to steal, but if your state doesn't do that, you can score your sticker with a pair of scissors or a razor. Cutting in diagonal strips is a popular method, and it deters thieves from stealing your inspection sticker.

Lug nut locks: In addition to license plates and license plate stickers, thieves like to steal car tires. They are easy to steal, easy to sell, not trackable, and, depending on the tires, the money can be good. One way to prevent this is to buy lug nut locks. When you buy a car, your dealer may offer this as an add-on, or you can buy them online and put them on yourself or take them to a mechanic, since they require a special tool. With a lug nut lock, you need at least one per wheel, or you can do all of the lug nuts on your wheels, but don't lose the key, because if you ever get a flat, you'll need that.

Some alternatives to lug nut locks include installing an alarm with a sensor that would detect if someone is trying to jack up your car. You can also park with your wheels turned at a forty-five-degree angle, which makes it harder for a thief to get the lug nuts off your wheel, as does parking close to the curb. These options aren't perfect, but they are free and offer some protection.

First aid kit: You can purchase a premade travel first aid kit for all the basics and then add what you feel is necessary. Here are a few extra items I like to include because the purchased kits either don't include them or don't have enough of them:

- **Extra adhesive bandages,** because you can never have enough. Whether it's your shoe giving you a blister or an actual cut, these are always nice to have on hand. They're great items to keep in your purse too.

- **Travel packs of basic medicines, like pain relievers.** You never know when a headache is going to strike, so I carry these in my purse too.

- **Extra cotton balls and cotton swabs,** which I keep in zippered plastic bags so that if I do need to apply some antibiotic ointment, I have a clean tool to use.

- **Extra gloves** because if I do need to treat an injury like a cut, I want to make sure I can protect myself from bodily fluids while also preventing infection. Additionally, if someone gets sick in your car and you have to clean up the mess, you'll be grateful to have gloves as a barrier.

- **Hand sanitizer.** I keep both the hand-wipe version and a pump bottle in my car. I like having options, and the wipes are really handy for cleaning a quick mess like spilled coffee in the cup holder. It'll get sticky and stinky if you don't clean it up quickly, so my wipes are always nearby. And here's a winter hack: hand sanitizer can also help de-ice car locks.

- **Paper cups.** These are useful for a variety of reasons. If you need to take some medicine or share water, the cups are great. If you see a stray animal and want to give it some water, you can fill up the cup or cut it down so it's easier for the animal to drink from. And this may seem extreme, but if you had to treat a puncture wound in an eye, you'd need to stabilize the protruding object, and a paper cup would allow you to do that while you sought emergency care. (This was one of those things I learned in a first aid course, and it has stuck with me forever— plus, it was in an episode of *Grey's Anatomy*.)

- **Scissors**—in case you need to cut the aforementioned paper cups, clothes, or simply forgot to take the tag off your new outfit.

- **Saline solution** for eye washing or cleaning a wound. If you don't have saline solution on hand, water can work, but it's not sterile, which is why it's best to use saline solution if you have it.

- **Cloths.** In the case of extreme injuries, you can keep some clean cloths in your car. If you have a head injury, you'd need something bigger than your average gauze pad or bandage, so that's when larger cloths are helpful. This isn't something you'd likely know how to use well unless you've taken a first aid course, so in case you haven't taken one, here's a tip on how to make these larger bandages. I went to my local thrift store and bought a set of sheets. When I got home, I cut the sheets down to the sizes I needed, washed them, dried them, and placed them in zippered bags to help them stay clean. Hopefully you'd never need these for an injury, but they're also helpful if you come across a stray animal or need to create a little pillow.

- **Duct tape** is universally practical, especially in a first aid kit. You could use it to make a quick bandage, splint, or sling; to remove a tick or splinter; or to prevent blisters in a pinch. Plus, if you need tape to reinforce a box you're mailing or attach the bumper back onto your car because you ran over the parking lot median, you'll be ready!

- **Resealable plastic bags.** I use these to keep tools clean and in case someone gets carsick, but in an emergency first aid situation, they can keep wounds clean as well as dry.

- **Diabetic emergency items.** No one in my household has diabetes, but in my first aid course, I learned the fifteen/fifteen rule, which states that in a diabetic emergency, someone should eat fifteen grams of fast-acting carbs and wait fifteen minutes. The fifteen grams of carbs can be anything from a glucose tablet to a juice box, granulated sugar, candy, soda, honey, or even cake frosting. I personally keep granulated sugar in my kit as an extra precaution because it can dissolve without a person having to chew it; plus, I don't have to worry about it leaking or melting in the car like juice or candy would.

Paper towels, napkins, and tissues: These are a must. In the glove compartment, I keep napkins with a travel tissue pack, and in my trunk, I have the paper towels. If there's ever a spill, I'm ready!

Feminine products: For those moments when you weren't expecting your time of the month to hit, but also for some first aid uses. Sanitary pads can be used on large wounds, and tampons can be used to absorb small blood flows, like a nosebleed. When using tampons, remember that they expand when absorbing liquid, so if it's in the nostril, it will expand and might hurt when it's time to pull the tampon out. Instead, I suggest keeping it at the edge of the nostril so it can absorb the blood without expanding inside of it.

A change of clothes: There is nothing worse than getting caught in the rain or spilling something on yourself when you still have a full day ahead, especially if you're at work. When I was commuting to an office, I'd keep a simple outfit in my car, like a black T-shirt and leggings, so I could dress it up or down in a pinch and hopefully avoid some awkward situations.

Sweater: Grandma always said to bring a sweater everywhere, and she was right. This might come from my Miami upbringing, but when it's hot outside and I walk into a mall or restaurant, it's always freezing. I can't handle that. It's uncomfortable and I will literally shiver if the temperature is below seventy degrees—hence, a sweater. Nothing fancy, just a simple sweater.

Umbrellas: Rain, rain, rain, and more rain. Maybe this is more of my Miami childhood showing itself, but I am always prepared for rain. In my car, I keep one or two large umbrellas and then two additional small ones. If I have guests in the car, I've got us covered. I like the small ones so I can throw them in my purse if I'm not sure what the weather will be like, and if I know it's going to pour, I have the larger umbrella.

Rubber flip-flops: I've ruined enough suede and leather shoes to learn to carry flip-flops with me. When I worked a corporate job, I'd keep a pair at work and a pair in my car. If I got caught in rain coming or going, it was no longer going to cost me hundreds in damaged shoes. You can do rain boots too, but they're bulky, so to save space, I turn to flip-flops instead. Also, if you ever decide to get a last-minute pedicure, you're prepared!

Pens and a notepad: These are very useful for quick note taking, and I don't know how many times I've caught myself writing last-minute greeting cards in the car on my way to a party. The pen and paper are essential for other practical reasons too. If you hit a car in a

parking lot and need to leave your contact information, a note on the windshield is the best way to do it. And if you witness a hit-and-run, you can jot down the information and leave it on the damaged car.

Pet rescue kit: I love animals, and growing up, I'd see a lot of strays, so I've always kept a kit in my car ready to rescue the next animal I came across. I have a small first aid kit that can be used for humans too, but for my pets I also keep a collar, a slip lead (a type of leash), a travel water bowl, and a few cans of cheap cat and dog food. The food can be used as bait so I can catch an animal, but if it's too scared and runs away, I at least leave the food behind and hope they'll find it. It's also useful if I come across someone struggling with houselessness who also has a pet.

My kit also includes an old towel because a lot of strays can have ticks or fleas, so I try to wrap them in the towel in an effort to contain that, or to simply keep my hands from getting bitten or scratched. I also use the towel (and at times gloves) as a bit of a barrier, since I don't know the state of an animal's health.

Bottle of water: No matter where I go, I always carry a bottle of water. If I don't have it, I immediately feel like I'm dying of thirst. I sleep with it, work with it, travel with it—my water bottle and I are inseparable. That said, I still keep a secondary water bottle in my car. I have it for  emergency situations in case I get stranded, need to rinse something off, or need to give someone a sip of water. If I come across a stray, I can use my first aid paper cups or travel water bowl to give it water. If I come across someone in need in general, I can give them the bottle of water, and if there's a spill in my car I need to rinse, I can again turn to my handy-dandy water bottle. There is a caveat, though: if you're parking in the hot summer sun for a prolonged period of time, the water inside a plastic bottle can become contaminated with high levels of BPA, and if it's been opened, bacteria can grow. This water can still be used for general cleaning, like rinsing bird poop off the car, but for human consumption, it's best to rotate your water bottle about every three weeks and keep it in a shady area. If the weather is cold, then you can get away with keeping it in your car much longer.

Plastic bags: In addition to the zippered plastic bags I keep in my first aid kit, I'll also include a couple of regular plastic bags. They can be used for garbage, dirty clothes, and in the winter, you can even use them to keep ice and snow from sticking to your side mirrors.

A red cloth, like a bandana or cleaning cloth: If you're stranded on the side of the road, a red flag or cloth signals to other drivers that you need help. Also, if you end up shopping for some larger items like furniture or hardware that stick out of your car, you're required to put a red-, yellow-, or orange-colored flag (or cloth) at the end of the load to help other drivers assess the depth so they can keep a safe distance. The requirements may vary based on your state, vehicle, and type of load, so check with your state's regulations.

Reusable tote bags: There are times when I need plastic bags, but otherwise, I hate having them pile up at home if I don't need them, so I always have my reusable eco-friendly totes with me. It's also much more comfortable to carry items on my shoulder with a tote bag than it is to carry them in a plastic bag around my wrist, particularly  if the items are heavy. If you're using the reusable totes for groceries, particularly meat, it's important to wash them after each use. According to a 2013 study led by the University of Arizona and Loma Linda University,[1] almost all of the reusable bags researchers randomly selected from customers entering a grocery store contained a significant number of bacteria, which in some cases included coliform and E. coli. If we wash or clean these tote bags after every use, we can help avoid cross contamination. If you're purchasing dry goods like pasta and using the tote bags for clothes, you can go several weeks—even up to two months—before washing them. Keep in mind that care instructions will vary based on the types of materials your bags are made with.

Snow shovel, windshield cover, and roof scraper: If you live in a place where it snows, you'll want to invest in some winter accessories for your car. A shovel is pretty obvious, but some more recent inventions are the large foam roof scrapers and the frost-free windshield guards. In my opinion, these items are safety aids for several reasons. I used to work nights and absolutely hated the idea of lingering in a parking lot late at night (or early in the morning) by myself. The winter was the only time when I had less control over this, because if my car got snowed in, I had to clear the snow before getting in my car, but these tools made that process faster so I wouldn't linger in the empty parking lot for very long. The tools I mentioned can help you get the snow off the roof of your car quickly and peel the snow from your front windshield in seconds. They're also made of materials that are safer for your car, so you won't accidentally scratch it. Also, because the tools make clearing the snow easier and faster, you're less likely to leave that snow piled on the roof of your car, which will not only get you a ticket in many places but can be distracting to other drivers and possibly obstruct their view.

A trunk organizer: Clearly, I keep a lot in my car, but my trunk is still incredibly functional thanks to my trunk organizer. Pretty much everything except my larger umbrellas fits right into my organizer, so if you have a phobia of clutter, I recommend it.

Seat belt cutter and window breaker: You may go your entire life without needing to break a car window, but there are a few emergency situations when you'll want to be prepared with tools for the circumstances. You could crash into water and your car could get submerged, or there could be an accident where you have to get out quickly but the door is blocked, or maybe you locked your keys in your car and your pet or child is also locked inside. Emergencies happen, so it's good to know how to deal with them when they do.

When I lived in Miami, it wasn't uncommon for me to hear of cars that had driven into canals. There are canals everywhere, so there are two thoughts that every Florida native has: (1) *Are there gators here?* and (2) *Can I survive a car accident where I land in a canal?* Respectively, the answers are probably and yes, but it's more likely that if you have a seat belt cutter and a window breaker—which are often sold as a combined tool—you will be able to escape quickly.

The key is keeping these items accessible to the driver of the car.

If it's in your glove compartment and your seat belt is locked tight, you may not be able to get to it. Similarly, it won't help you if it's in your trunk. You can keep it on the side of the driver's door, in the center console, on the sun visor, or better yet, there are versions of this tool that lock right onto your seat belt and stay there permanently in case you need it.

You'll also want to look for a seat belt cutter that doesn't allow the seat belt to curl as it's being cut, which will make it harder to slice through, and you'll want a tool that protects you from coming into contact with the blade in everyday situations. There are lots of online videos reviewing these products and testing them on junkyard cars, so you can see which ones best suit your needs.

And while we're talking about breaking a car window in an emergency, if you're stuck inside a car and need to break the window to exit, your instinct will likely be to hit the center of the glass, but that's actually the strongest point. Ideally, you want to start by striking at the corners of the glass—and choose the window closest to you. Also, don't forget to call emergency services. It's nice to have a plan of attack while you wait for them to arrive, but the sooner you can call them, the better.

If you don't have a window-breaking tool available, here are some other tools you can use, although I'd still recommend an emergency window-breaking tool:

- **A removable headrest:** Not every car's headrest is removable, so check your front and back seats to see if your car has this functionality. You can try striking the window at a weak point, or take the metal pegs and jam them toward the bottom of the window in the door panel. Once you have the pegs down as far as possible, pull the headrest toward you until you hear a snap, and the glass should crack. This isn't easy to do, and it's not the most efficient way to break a car window, but if you have nothing else available, it's worth trying.

- **Ceramic spark plugs:** This only works if you're outside the car and happen to have access to spark plugs, but if you slam a ceramic spark plug onto a hard surface like the asphalt of a parking lot, you should get a shard of ceramic. If sharp enough and thrown with enough force at a car window, the impact of the shard will create a tiny structural failing that will cause the window to break. Keep in mind that in some states it's illegal to walk around with spark plug shards.

- **A claw hammer:** This is a tool you can keep in your car, or if you have an emergency outside a car, someone around you may have one. It's a basic hammer, but you can use the claw side to try to crack the glass. As with a window breaker, strike the edges of the window first, because those are the weakest points and, thus, are most likely to break. Again, this isn't easy, but with enough repetition and force, you might be successful.

General rules for breaking car windows:

- The driver and passenger windows are designed differently than the front and rear windshields. In an emergency situation, your go-to point of contact should be the weakest windows, which are the side windows.

- If you're in the vehicle, break the window closest to you, but if you're outside the vehicle and trying to break in because your child or pet is locked inside, choose the window farthest away from them. Remember, as the glass breaks, it can shatter, and you want to protect them from the broken glass if possible.

  Breaking a car window will differ from model to model. Some cars have laminated glass windows, in which case the glass will crack but will remain together due to a plastic layer that's baked between the two pieces of glass. You can look up your car's make and model to see which windows of your car (if any) have laminated glass. With laminated glass, the aforementioned tools won't be effective.

Blind spot mirrors: If your car doesn't have blind spot mirrors and sensors built in, getting them is an absolute must. As with most of the tools mentioned in this book, they're affordable and easy to install, while improving your safety on the road. The National Highway Traffic Safety Administration reports that more than eight hundred thousand accidents happen every year due to blind spots.[2] Whether we're changing lanes or parking, blind spot mirrors can help us prevent accidents while also providing some general benefits, like helping us keep an eye on how close we are to the curb.

When choosing a blind spot mirror, there are a lot of different sizes and options. You'll want to make sure you get one that's small so it doesn't take up a lot of room on your side mirrors but still allows you to see your blind spot. Also, I prefer the blind spot mirrors on a swivel, so I can adjust the angle as needed, and ones that are made of a durable material like aluminum. Keep in mind that depending on where you live and how you store your car, it may be worth spending a few extra dollars for a longer lasting material such as aluminum.

And by the way, whether you lease or own your car, you can still install blind spot mirrors. They're easy to remove if needed, but follow any directions that come with the mirrors you purchase. In my case, I typically use a razor blade to carefully remove the adhesive from the side mirror, and I do it slowly, so the blade doesn't scratch the glass. If there's any leftover adhesive, I use rubbing alcohol to remove it.

Snacks: The quintessential Mom Friend is always loaded with packaged snacks. I may not have snacks in my car at all times, but if I'm driving thirty minutes away and there's a chance I'll get stuck in heavy traffic or be stranded in a storm, or if I'm with friends headed to a club, then I know to stock up on snacks. My go-to snacks are granola bars, fruit-leather bars, jerky, and crackers or pretzels.

Weird things on the windshield: This isn't something you'd carry with you, but it's worth noting because there are a ton of viral safety videos warning of people being targeted with things on their windshields. It could be zip ties, clothes, a doll, or letters written in the dust or snow. In all of the cases I've come across, the origins of the stories were myths, and no official warnings were issued by police. That said, even if it's just a mischievous person messing around and leaving things on your car, it's still scary. If you're ever on the road and are uncomfortable by something found on your car, don't reason with yourself about how it could be a hoax. We talked about listening to our gut in a previous section, so if you're uncomfortable, don't talk yourself out of it. Depending on where you are, you can ask for an escort to walk you to your car or get in your car quickly and cautiously drive somewhere safe in order to take the item off your windshield.

That said, when you see these scary viral videos or posts, stop to do a little extra digging before sharing. I've seen some misinformation get shared that is incredibly dangerous. For example, one post urged people that if they're on a highway in the United States and have an emergency, not to call 911 but instead call some other emergency number. That is absolutely false—911 is the universal number in the United States.

The spread of misinformation applies to any subject, and safety is certainly included in that statement! If I'm watching something that elicits a primal reaction like fear or anger, that's my red flag to look into it a bit more deeply. Luckily, it's very easy to verify information nowadays. I turn to my trusty search engine, type in a few key words like *zip ties on windshield wipers crime*, click Enter, and in less than a second, I get hundreds of news articles and police announcements debunking the myth.

Again, if you ever feel uncomfortable, listen to your gut, but don't let other people scare you needlessly. They're just in it for the clickbait.

Car tracker: Car trackers are small tracking devices you can purchase for your car, particularly if you park on the street. I use an AirTag for my car, so if it's ever stolen, I can track it. You can also put devices like this on bicycles, dog collars, and more. They're small, affordable, and easy to use. If you have an Apple device, it should alert you that an AirTag is traveling with you, and for Android devices there are apps to help you identify sneaky AirTags. Pay attention to these to make sure that no one has stolen your vehicle.

Driving a Car: Safety First

I won't discuss general road safety rules, because my guess is if you have a driver's license, you're already familiar with the basics. Instead, this section will focus on the bad habits that may put us at risk without our realizing it.

Car decals: Police have warned against sharing too much information on your car. I'm sure that you either have or have seen stickers that advertise where your children go to school, the local sports teams you're a part of, your church, the size of your family, the name of your dog, and more. Some people even get vanity plates with their names on them. While these are generally harmless, in the wrong hands, they could provide key pieces of information as to where you hang out or where to find your family, and they can even be used to build rapport with you in order to get close to you or your loved ones. Some decals are riskier than others, but before putting these on a car, think, *Is this something I want to be public?* If you wouldn't walk into a mall and announce it, don't put it on your car.

Parking decals: As with hobby and family decals, parking decals often get overlooked. We're often required to use the decal for our apartment buildings, schools, and jobs. If the decal just has a number with no other identifying information, it's probably fine, but if it says "West Elm High No. 432," then that's not something I'd want advertised on my car. Now, because they're often required in order to park at certain schools, residences, and jobs, I put the sticker on a clear CD case instead of sticking it on my car window. When I park, I put the case on my dashboard, and when I'm out and about, I remove it. In my case, I've never had an administrative team complain about my bending the rules, but should it come up, I'd explain the safety concern using words like *liability* (every business's nightmare). To be clear, I'm talking about a civilized conversation, not a viral Karen moment. *Insert cliche about catching more flies with honey than vinegar here.*

Parking safety: Here are a few steps we can take that help us stay safe while parking.

- **Always lock your doors:** The moment you get into a car, your doors should be locked. If you're driving down the block from your house, lock your door. Running into a restaurant to grab takeout? Lock the car. Pumping gas? Lock the car. Cars get stolen all the time because people leave them unlocked. And this isn't based on whether or not you're in a good neighborhood—it's a crime of convenience. While traveling abroad, I've also heard stories of thieves running up to cars stopped at a red light and stealing goods inside the car. I don't know how often this happens or where, but keeping the doors locked would certainly help in that situation as well.

- **Roll up your windows:** Whenever you're parked, stuck in traffic, or traveling along local roads where you're stopping a lot, it's safest to keep the windows up. That fresh air may be nice on a highway, but if there are pedestrians around, you take the risk that one of them may want to grab something from your car or harass you.

- **Keep valuables out of sight:** Loose change, charging cables, shopping bags, or packages (even if they're empty)—when you're parked, hide all of those items. From the window, you want your car to look clean and empty in order to prevent tempting the wandering thief who is looking for an opportunity. Sure, they can break a window, but unless they're on a car-destruction rampage, they generally peek through the window and check to see if the car is locked, and at that point they may move on to an easier target unless there's something they really want inside. I personally like to hide anything valuable in the trunk of the car or in the center console or glove compartment if the item is small enough, but sometimes I'll also hide things under a seat or even under a sweater.

- **Keep mail out of sight:** If you're mailing packages, picking up mail from a PO Box, or have magazines in the car with your address on them, put them away or, if you're in a rush, flip them over so the address isn't visible. For thieves in the business of identity theft, envelopes may be tempting if they think they contain identity information. But I also worry about the random creep I may come across while running errands. That person might walk away, or they might go inspect your car while you're grocery shopping and find an address to stalk. Or maybe you have an uneasy confrontation with someone who seems like they're not above revenge or harassment; you don't want to put your address right in their view. I can't say if these things ever happen on the reg, but if I can think of them, so can someone else, and it only takes a moment to hide that personal information.

- **Park in well-lit areas:** As I mentioned in chapter 1, good lighting has been shown to reduce crime. If parking in a well-lit area is available, always choose the light. Similarly, you'll want to park as close to the entrance of your destination as possible.

- **Park in populated areas:** If you can avoid it, try to stay away from desolate areas. It's best to park your car near other cars in high trafficked areas, and near popular entry and exit paths so you can avoid being alone in a parking lot.

- **Spare keys:** Keep your spare keys at home, not in your car. If they're in the car, they will be found.

- **Garage door openers:** If you're not parking in the garage, bring the garage door opener inside with you. In fact, bring it with you no matter where you are (if it's not built into the car), because if someone breaks into your vehicle, they can theoretically use the garage door opener to easily gain access to your home. If you keep your car insurance card or have pieces of mail in your car, it's even easier for them to find the address. Even if that wasn't originally their plan, having the garage door opener in the car might be tempting enough.

- **Awareness:** As always with personal safety, awareness is key. Don't be afraid to take notice of who and what is around you as you walk confidently to your destination.

- **Look inside:** I don't know how this habit started, but so many women look in their cars before getting back into them, particularly at gas stations. There's a fear that as you're distracted, someone might hop into the back seat. Some women may have even been taught this in driver's education, and it's not a bad idea. Being aware of what's in and around our vehicles or us in general is a good habit to get into.

- **Don't linger:** When you're returning to your vehicle, don't linger. Don't leave your passenger door open as you're looking for something in the trunk. Don't chat on the phone as you're bringing groceries into and out of the house, leaving all the doors wide open and/or unlocked. When you're headed to your car, do it with purpose. Have your keys ready to go in your hand, get in the car, lock the doors, put your seat belt on, start the engine, and get moving. There's no need to hang out in the parking lot by yourself if you don't have to.

- **Use the tools available to you:** Your phone, safety apps, smart safety jewelry, and more are all available to you to use when you're feeling vulnerable. If you're heading back to a parking lot late at night, that's the perfect time to remind yourself that you have these safety devices to rely on should something happen.

Parking in reverse: Believe it or not, reverse parking is safer than pulling in headfirst. When we're backing out of a parking spot, there are a ton of blind spots; plus, our vision is restricted because of the cars and objects around us. According to the National Highway Traffic Safety Administration, an estimated 267 people are killed and 15,000 injured each year by drivers backing out of parking spots, and it's usually in parking lots and driveways.[3] By parking in reverse, you have better visibility of pedestrians and any oncoming traffic. Fortunately, newer vehicles also have back-up cameras and sensors that help reduce the risk of these accidents.

I know personally how useful these are. A few years ago, I ran into a café to grab a coffee. I was parked headfirst in a small parking lot—it only had about eight parking spots—and as I was backing out, my new car suddenly jolted me to a stop. My foot was on the gas, I was in reverse gear, but the car stopped me because a sensor caught motion behind the car, which I couldn't see in the back-up camera. Then a woman came to my driver's window thanking me for stopping because her little girl had gotten away from her and run behind my car. I told her not to thank me but the car manufacturer, because I hadn't seen her in the camera or my rearview mirror; she had run through a blind spot, and if it weren't for my car's sensors, I probably would've hit her.

There are times when we can't park in reverse, but when you can, it's a simple way to increase safety. Also, if there is an emergency, I find that I'm able to get into my vehicle much faster and drive straight out, as opposed to when I've parked headfirst.

Key fob hack: If your car has an alarm and the button is on the key fob, you can use this as a personal or even a home alarm. Let's say you're getting out of work late at night or you have a late-night class. Walking back to your car, you can set off the alarm to scare anyone who might be hanging out near your vehicle, or if someone did approach you in the parking lot, you can use it as a personal alarm to call attention to yourself. Some people also sleep with their car's key fob on the nightstand, because if they hear a suspicious noise outside their home, like someone walking through the bushes, they can set off their car alarm as a deterrent. Of course, it's not linked to emergency services the way a traditional alarm system would be, but anyone who's up to mischief generally doesn't want to be caught, and a high-pitched alarm doesn't help their cause.

Safe driving distance: While on the road, keeping a safe distance from the cars around you isn't just useful if you need to suddenly stop. Car accidents happen every day, but sometimes these accidents are staged to commit insurance fraud. According to the National Insurance Crime Bureau, the victims of these crimes are usually women and senior citizens who are driving alone, because they're thought to be less con-frontational.[4] Also, new vehicles, rentals, and commercial vehicles are more often targeted because they're likely well insured. One of the most common scams is called the "swoop and squat." There are a variety of tactics used to run the scam, and there are usually a few bad actors in-volved, but basically your car gets boxed in while on a freeway so you can't change lanes, and then the car in front of you suddenly hits the brakes, forcing you to hit the back of it. Afterward, everyone in that car will claim injuries, and because you drove into them, it's presumed to be your fault. One way to prevent this is to keep enough distance between you and the car in front of you so that you can't be boxed in. This applies while driving on any road, even when you're stopped at a stop sign or red light. If you're ever in an accident, call the police immediately and take videos as well as photos if you can. Dashcams are helpful here as well (more on this in a moment).

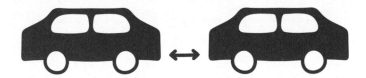

Road scams: While we're on the topic of staged accidents, here are a few other bad actors to be aware of.

- Runners and cappers. These are people who suddenly appear at an accident scene, trying to get you to use a specific doctor or attorney. They're usually part of a criminal scheme.

- Doctors who insist you file a personal injury claim after an accident, even if you're not hurt. In general, if anyone is being too persistent, that's a red flag.

- Tow trucks that show up at the scene of an accident, even though you didn't call for their service.

- There are also door-to-door "repairmen" that'll scan neighborhoods for damaged cars and claim to be able to fix dents or other damages. I was targeted by this kind of scam when I was sixteen. My car had a slight dent in the rear door, and a "repairman" offered assistance. I told him I'd take his information because I only had twenty dollars on me. He said that was enough and, without permission, began working on my car with a tool that stuck holes all along the side where the dent was. When I insisted that I really didn't want the work done, he ran off. I was timid at the time and was trying to nicely tell him that I didn't want any service at the moment. I don't even remember if I had paid him anything—I may have, just to get him to leave— but I do remember being very upset. Lesson learned. So, I advise you that if anyone offers unsolicited help, a clear and assertive no is the best way to go.

Dashcams: Dashcams are a fun way of recording long trips, but they can also be incredibly useful if you need evidence of a road scam, are a parent of a young driver, drive a commercial vehicle, or maybe you just want a little protection while on the road in case of an accident. Some dashcams even have extra features like the ability to record even when the car is off and send you an alert if anything is amiss. Whatever your reason may be, a dashcam can be a helpful tool.

Car computer settings: Many vehicles have computer settings that you can adjust, and the one I've found to be the most useful for safety is the control for how the car doors unlock. On my vehicle, I'm able to select whether I want all of my car doors to unlock at once or if I only want the driver's door to unlock. The functionality may be limited depending on the vehicle, but it's worth playing with your car's settings to look for safety features, particularly if you have a newer vehicle.

Valet parking tip: Your car likely has some features to protect your valuables when you use valet parking. One feature is called valet mode, and it's found in some newer vehicles, but first let's talk about your car's key fob. Your key fob likely has a mechanical key built in. It can unlock the car in case your key fob's battery runs out, but that same key can also lock or unlock your glove compartment. In newer vehicles, that glove compartment box might contain a valet mode button, which, when engaged, locks the glove compartment and the trunk of the car (typically sedans). The purpose of this is so that you can hide valuables like luggage if you're traveling. You just give your key fob to the valet attendant and take the mechanical key with you. The car will drive and function normally (although for some high-end vehicles, valet mode also limits speed), but it prevents a stranger from snooping around your trunk and glove compartment. To undo the mode, you simply unlock your glove compartment box, click the valet mode button to disengage, and everything is back to normal.

This is typically a feature found in newer luxury vehicles; however, for several decades, car manufacturers have been producing glove compartments with a lock. So, if your key fob has a removable mechanical key, you should be able to lock smaller valuables in your glove compartment when you use valet parking or for other reasons. Also, check the car manual packet that's often stored in the glove compartment when you buy a new car. In some cases, your spare key may be stored in that box, which makes for a quick getaway if a thief were to find it.

CHAPTER 5

MOM FRIEND IS PACKED: TRAVEL SMART

I caught the travel bug early on. I've been flying alone since I was a preteen. My aunt worked for a public school system, and since she always had her summers off, I'd join her for trips throughout the US and Canada, sometimes traveling to meet her by myself. We'd fly, drive, take overnight trains—we always made it a point to try every type of transportation available just to experience it. Years later, I still love to travel. I've taken at least one major trip just about every year since I was a teenager, and I've been to big cities like Paris as well as remote villages in the Amazon. I've traveled solo and with friends and family, and I'm a big fan of larger group tours when available.

I mention this because in all my years of travel, having visited more than thirty different countries, I have generally felt safe. The most common incidents I have encountered are scams and theft, which are inconvenient, but I wasn't afraid for my safety. For example, in one instance, while I was traveling with friends, we noticed we had been targeted by a group of young men for what I believed was theft. They had been following us around a public plaza on motorcycles (a quick getaway vehicle like a bike or motorcycle is a red flag), but because we caught on, my friends and I went into a hotel, sat at the bar for a few hours, and waited for them to pass. When we came back out, they were gone.

The reason I've felt safe while traveling? Mom Friend–esque preparation. I'm prepared to get robbed and I'm prepared to lose luggage.

I do a lot of research ahead of time, and I use tools available to me to stay safe. In this chapter, I'll let you in on everything I've learned while traveling abroad so you can use some of these tips on your next adventure.

Research, research, research: Whether you're traveling domestically or abroad, before booking anything, look into the details of your destination online. Are there neighborhoods you should avoid? (The short answer here is yes—no matter where you are, there are parts that are safe and parts that aren't.) What are common local scams? Local emergency numbers? If abroad, are there visa entry requirements? Recommended vaccines? Are there any travel warnings? Where's your embassy, if the country that you're traveling to has one? Can you take out cash at your destination or are you required to bring everything with you in advance? (For most countries, this may not apply, but there are a few nations where this is the case. For example, in Cuba, you can't access US dollars on the island, so you have to come prepared with all the cash you'll need for the entire trip beforehand, including any emergency cash.) The more prepared you are, the less likely you'll be thrown for a loop should something go wrong.

Register with the embassy: In the United States, travel registration is a free service for US citizens who are traveling to or living in a foreign country. (I'm sure there are other countries with similar programs, but as I'm only familiar with the US program, I'll use that as my example.) The program is called the Smart Traveler Enrollment Program, and it allows the embassy to help you quickly in the case of an emergency. When you enroll, you'll provide the embassy with details such as the length of your stay, your itinerary, and even relevant medical information (optional). If there's a natural disaster, terrorism, or civil unrest, the embassy can help locate you to bring you to safety. Also, if you're a victim of a crime or an accident, or if you become ill, the embassy can help you find your way back home. If you're traveling to a place that doesn't have an embassy, consulate, or a "foreign interests section" for your country, know that there is an added risk, and you may want to reconsider the trip.

Also worth noting is that the US has a twenty-four-hour consular emergency hotline. If you're traveling, you should keep that number close. You can keep a copy in your passport, on your phone, and in your luggage. In case you get robbed or your luggage goes missing, you'll want a few backup copies.

Make copies of your travel documents: The US Department of State recommends you photocopy your passport information and take one copy on your trip with you (don't store it in the same place as your passport) and leave another copy behind with a trusted friend or family member. I take it one step further. I'll photocopy my driver's license and passport, carry a printed copy with me, leave one at home with family, email a version to myself or save it in a cloud backup, and keep a photo of it on my  phone. Once I return from my trip, I delete the emails and photos in case of a hack, but while traveling, I like the idea of having several ways to access important travel documents.

The reason you want to do this is because should you lose your travel documents, or if someone steals them, it'll be much easier to get a replacement if you have proof of your identity. You would have to contact your nearest consulate or embassy to obtain a replacement, which is why it's also good to know where that is in relation to where you're traveling to.

Communicate: Share your plans with trusted friends or family back home so they know where you're expected to be. Whether you're the type of person who plans every minute of an itinerary or you prefer to go with the flow, share your plans with someone back home (and your nearest embassy). This should include your flight information, accommodations, any other booked travel, and general plans for the day. Should an emergency arise, knowing where you're supposed to be will help those concerned about you locate you.

Get familiar with common scams: Whether domestic or abroad, scams are everywhere. There's the street shoeshine cons, the fake silent monks asking for donations, rogue taxicabs, and countless other ploys. With these street scams, the criminals are after one thing—cash—but when they don't get what they want, they can become aggressive, and you're often outnumbered, leaving you in a vulnerable position where you may fear for your safety. An easy rule of thumb is that if you're approached, walk away. There are certainly exceptions. For example, when I see Girl Scouts selling cookies, I'm stopping, and same goes for the Salvation Army Santas. These are well-established traditions, but if I'm approached by someone I'm unfamiliar with, I immediately say I'm not interested and walk away. Here are a few common scams you're likely to come by in your travels, but this list isn't exhaustive, so before you head out to your next destination, take a moment to go online and look up the common scams for that area.

- **Unofficial transit tickets:** You may come across people selling bus or train tickets outside transit stations (usually near an airport, where it's easy to spot tourists). They'll promise it's discounted or that you get a free ride, but that's all fake. Only purchase transit tickets from the designated machines or authorized tellers.

- **Being offered a taxi:** You can order a taxi from an app like Uber or Lyft, or you can wait in a designated taxi line, which most airports have. When you travel to smaller destinations such as islands, a small village in the Amazon, or a remote part of Italy, the rules get blurred. Transit in these areas may rely on unofficially marked vehicles, which further emphasizes why it's important to look up the common scams ahead of time. If you're near an airport, port, or transit station, you can also ask an attendant for assistance—there's usually someone nearby to help.

- **Fake event or tourist-destination tickets:** This one is well-known. I haven't seen as much of it as I used to now that more and more venues are using app-based sales, but still be on the lookout for people selling entrance tickets outside venues. It can feel like a deal, but unless they're walking with you to the gate to scan the ticket so you can ensure it's legit before you pay, the only way you should buy tickets is from the venue itself or an authorized website that will guarantee your money back, like Ticketmaster or StubHub.

- **Street photos:** If you take a photo with a street character or an animal, know that a tip is expected. Tip at least a dollar for a quick photo (or something equivalent in the local currency). In New York City, for instance, street characters, while not official mascots, are accepted as independent workers who earn all their money off tourist tips. It's not exactly a scam, but if you're unaware that tipping is essentially required, then it can feel like one. When I was in Peru, I took a photo with a baby llama on the street, and although I tipped, the owners were upset I didn't tip more. I didn't have any smaller bills, and fortunately, they weren't aggressive, but it's a risk that you should know you're taking when you want a street photo. The saving grace is that usually this happens in popular tourist destinations that have a solid police presence, so it feels safer.

  Another version of this scam is the unofficial photographers offering to take your photo at a popular tourist destination. They'll take the photos with their cameras but when they ask for payment, it's expensive. You're better off asking another tourist nearby to take a photo of you. As an alternative, someone may approach you, offering to take a photo of you with your camera or phone, and then they run off with your valuables. As a general rule, if you ask someone for help, you're unlikely to select a criminal, so always ask for help versus accepting unsolicited help.

- **Shoe/shoeshine scam:** I've come across this in a few places, but most often in New Orleans. The vendors will make a comment about your shoes, such as, "Bet ten dollars I can tell you where you got your shoes," or they get down and start shining your shoes without asking, and the next thing you know, you owe them forty dollars. They're often in groups, too, so it's intimidating if you don't give in. Generally, I can spot these ahead of time (these folks have a swag about them), and I'll cross the street to avoid them if I can. If I can't, I say, "No, thank you," and keep walking. Do not engage.

- **Fake Buddhist monks:** This one is common in NYC, but there have been reports of this scam from as far away as Australia. A man in an orange robe will hand you a card to read or a medallion and ask for donations for a cause. If you don't pay up, they can also get aggressive. If someone approaches you handing you something, generally it's best not to take it. The exception would be a junky post-card advertisement or restaurant menu, in which case you simply may not want it.

- **The fake take-out menu:** A flyer for a restaurant gets slipped under your hotel door. You call to order food and hand over your credit card information, but you'll never get anything to eat. Instead, they'll use or sell your credit card information. If you get a menu under your door, you can call the hotel front desk to confirm it's real and look up the restaurant online. Also, you can pay cash or order through a trusted food delivery app, and you'll avoid the problem altogether.

- **Street games:** Whether it's three-card monte or the cup/shell game popular in Europe, these types of ploys are a common street scam. They are usually operated by a gang of people: one person is shuffling cards, another is playing, a few people are spectators, and another looks out for police. Their skilled sleight of hand will make it nearly impossible for you to pick the right cup or card, but even if you do, they'll signal another player to outbid you, scream, "Police!" and run off, or have someone pick your pockets while you're distracted.

- **Medical marijuana card scam:** This is a newer scam, but in places where medical marijuana cards are legal, you may see signs advertising cards for forty dollars. When you go in, they'll ask for your ID, you'll fill in some forms, consult with a "doctor," and then you find out that the forty dollars was only for the consult—if you want the card, it's a few hundred dollars more. If you refuse to pay, there's a chance you may not get your ID back. Avoid these.

- **Unofficial parking attendants:** Depending on where you are, this could be a scam, or it could be part of daily life. Once, while in downtown Miami, I was directed to park in a lot by a guy who then gave me a price, I gave him a twenty-dollar bill, he said he was going to get change, and then he ran off with my money. Turns out he wasn't the attendant and I had to pay a different guy to park my car. Look for attendants in uniform, get a parking ticket, and pay at the booth.

Another version of this con is one you must pay into. When traveling abroad, there are cities where you'll be asked to pay someone to "watch" your car. You'll park in a public spot and someone will approach you, asking you to tip them to keep an eye on your car. If you don't pay, you may come back to a damaged vehicle. In parts of Peru, this is a common practice, and I will often look for the guys to pay them if they don't see me, because I don't want to come back to a scratched-up car. It's usually a few dollars, similar to what you'd tip a valet.

- **ATM skimming:** Skimming is an illegal activity where a criminal will install a device on an ATM that records bank account data, and when you enter your PIN code, they steal that too. There are a few signs that an ATM has been messed with—most notably, there could be a hidden camera, and a skimmer itself is usually installed right over the card reader and curves outward. If you pull on it or look closely, you may notice the ATM has been tampered with. Another sign is a keypad overlay. If there's no hidden camera, this is an alternative method to record your PIN.

  To avoid this scam, choose ATMs at controlled environments like a bank. Before approaching the ATM, look to see if there are any suspicious characters, and as you approach it, look for signs of a rigged ATM. Also, at any ATM, rigged or not, cover your PIN while typing it in. You can also set up SMS notifications with your bank so that you'll get a text anytime there's a transaction on your card (you can specify when you get notified so it's not every time you use your card), and when you travel, you can also use a separate bank account and change your PIN after your trip. Pro tip: Don't use the last four digits of your phone number as your ATM PIN code. If the scammer pulled your name from a rigged ATM, it takes seconds to find your phone number online and guess the PIN. Remember, in the US, most information like phone numbers, emails, and addresses are publicly available online unless you actively try to get that information deleted, which takes vigilance (see chapter 3 if you missed how to do this and why it's so important).

- **Snatch thefts:** These happen in a variety of ways: someone could have watched you pull money out of an ATM, or they can ask for your phone to make an emergency call and run off with it. Of course, if you're distracted in public, you're more likely to become a victim of a snatch theft, whether the robber takes off with your phone, purse, or backpack. This happens everywhere, but a few signs I've noticed is that the criminals like to be on bicycles or motorcycles. When you're crossing the street or standing near a corner, they'll grab what's in your hand and they're able to take off quickly because they're on an easy-to-maneuver vehicle. Whenever I see a group of riders on bikes, I'm on alert and valuables stay close.

  The bikes are my biggest concern, but there are a few other methods for this scam too. If you're driving and keep your purse on the passenger seat, someone can open your door and grab it (always keep your doors locked). If you like to hook your purse on the back of your chair whenever you're out and about in public, that's another easy target. Keep your valuables close, and you can even buy antitheft bags that can be locked onto objects to make them harder to snatch. Also, while this happens everywhere, be on high alert when you're in crowded hotspots.

- **Romance scams:** You're probably familiar with the fake catfish profiles that scam people online, but romance scams can develop in person as well. It could be someone who works at a hotel, restaurant, or, most frequently in my experience, in a club. If you go to one abroad, sit back and watch as the sharks descend. It's incredible. In Cuba I went into a club with four girlfriends, and within minutes, they had all been taken into a corner by a *jinetero*, a man who is basically a prostitute but who sometimes also builds a flirtatious friendship in the hope that the relationship can continue when the person goes back to their country, after which the man then convinces the person to pay for some of his bills or to send money. (Women who do this are called *jineteras*.) Sometimes these professionals even have several girlfriends or boyfriends abroad sending them money. This can happen anywhere. If you're like the girls I went to Cuba with, you might have fun with the attention and then it ends there, but for others, deeper feelings develop, and that's when it hurts the most. Not only because you get scammed for cash but accepting you've been used and then breaking off a relationship you thought was real is incredibly painful.

- **The friendship bracelet scam:** I've seen this most frequently in Paris. This scam can take on a few forms. Someone might ask you if you want a friendship bracelet or ring, and if you say yes, they'll tie the bracelet or ring on so tight that it's impossible to remove, and the only way to get it off is by giving them money. They might also ask if you want to see a magic trick, then proceed to tie a string around your wrist. If you accept, they'll demand payment, and sometimes they can get aggressive and grab your arm after you've said no. If that happens, scream, "Don't touch me!" (preferably in the local language), and they'll almost certainly run away. This is also where a personal alarm might be helpful.

- **Petition scam:** A scammer, often pretending to be deaf or mute, will ask you to sign a petition for a cause, requesting your name, email, and a donation amount. The donation amount is usually filled out ahead of time, and it's high. If you don't pay, you'll be harassed, and an accomplice might steal from you while you're distracted.

- **Free rose scam:** Nothing is free. If you're lucky, when someone hands you a "free" rose, it's only because they're filming it for social media to gain likes, but often it's a scam. More frequently, you'll be offered a rose from a woman, a child, or a man, and naturally, they'll want money for it if you accept. You can walk away after recognizing the scam, give it back (although you might be met with resistance), or, if you're feeling generous, you can buy the rose.

- **The gold ring scam:** A person, often a woman, will pick up a gold ring on the street and ask if you dropped it. While she's talking to you, her "team" will pick your pockets.

- **Currency exchange scam:** Never exchange money on the street; go only to authorized money exchange venues such as banks, hotels, or malls that have currency exchange offices. Also, ask in advance what the rate is and how much money you're going to get. Another option is to stick to bank ATMs, and then you'll know you're getting the official rate. On the street, you can be fooled with fake currency since, as a tourist, you're unlikely to notice the differences. Con artists can also use a rigged calculator to come up with any number, and they'll use unfavorable exchange rates.

- **Stain scam:** This is a common pickpocket tactic that you may have even seen in movies. Someone will purposely spill something like mustard or ketchup on you. Then someone else will point it out and offer you a tissue; as you clean it up, they'll pick your pockets and steal anything they can get their hands on. If someone offers to help with your stain, politely refuse and head to a nearby restaurant or hotel to handle it on your own.

- **Drug scam:** When traveling, you might be offered drugs by a cabdriver or by random locals. When the deal is about to go down, a fake policeman arrives, demanding you pay to avoid jail time. To avoid this, don't do anything that's considered illegal in the country where you're traveling to. Make sure you know the customs and laws ahead of time.

BLEND IN

This is one of the most important tips. When traveling, whether part of a group or solo, it's important to blend in. You're less likely to be targeted for a scam or anything else if you dress like a local. I know we want to look glam for the 'Gram, but think about whether it's appropriate. If I'm headed to Miami Beach or spending a day in New York City, I'm comfortable enough to wear my jewelry and not feel like a target, but when I'm traveling abroad, I'm out of my comfort zone, so I'll avoid wearing flashy jewelry (even if it's fake) and designer clothing or carrying expensive bags or luggage. I also recommend avoiding personalized items, like a backpack with your name on it. Someone can use that information to act as if they know you and distract you while someone else picks your pockets. When I travel, I like to wear a cheap watch with a rubber athletic band. This helps me tell time throughout the day without having to take out an expensive smartphone, and because it's a thin athletic band, it's hard to mistake for a more expensive watch.

I also tend to stick to muted clothes—namely, gray, black, and white T-shirts, and jeans or leggings. Depending on the length of the trip, I'll bring two outfits that can be dressed up for a night out; everything else is casual but not touristy. I'll also scroll through Instagram and check out destinations where I'm traveling to see what people are wearing. Avoid checking travel brochures for this—those are often Photoshopped.

If you're a photo enthusiast, consider changing the strap on your fancy camera so it doesn't advertise the brand name. You can get a crossbody strap and hide your camera under a jacket so it's still accessible but not visible. You can also stash it in an antitheft bag and take it out as needed—it just depends on the trip and how often you'll be taking photos. For instance, on a safari, my camera is around my neck, but when I'm on a bus in Peru, it's hidden away.

Also, avoid wearing all the traditional tourist souvenir T-shirts. For example, sporting a T-shirt with the name of the city you're visiting plastered across the front is like wearing a sign that lets everyone know you're from out of town and probably a first-time visitor. A massive backpack is another giveaway. Sometimes you can't avoid a huge backpack, but try to consolidate by only bringing the essentials with you. You can travel with a smaller, more fashionable backpack, but avoid those giant ones if possible.

MINIMIZE VALUABLES

Aside from minimizing the valuables I wear, I also minimize the cash and cards I travel with. I do this whether I'm going to the local bar on a Friday night or traveling throughout Europe. I'll carry some cash, an ATM card, a credit card, an ID, health insurance cards, and if I'm traveling abroad, my passport. Should my bag get lost or stolen, at least I know exactly what's in my bag so I can act quickly to report lost cards and order replacements. I'll also take photos of what I'm traveling with and the phone numbers on the back of the credit cards, because in case my wallet is lost or stolen, I can quickly cancel any cards.

As a backup, I also have my smartphone enabled with an e-wallet feature (not travel specific) in case I forget or lose my wallet. That way I can still get some essentials while I wait for a replacement. I also split my cash up. If I have $600 in cash for my trip, I might carry $100 to $150 on me (depending on what the plans are for the day), and I leave the rest in the hotel safe. (If the hotel doesn't have a safe, there are alternatives, which I will detail later in this chapter.) Also, with the cash I might carry on me, I don't keep it all in my wallet. I'll keep some in my wallet, some in another zipper in my purse, some in a zippered scrunchie or money belt, and maybe some in my shoe or a jeans pocket. I do this for a few reasons: theft is an obvious one, but also, if I'm negotiating with street vendors, I don't want to show all my cards. If I say I only have twenty dollars on me, I want to be able to open my wallet and show only twenty dollars. I'll hide money throughout my wallet, purse, and person for safety but also to help stretch my dollar while traveling.

ALWAYS HAVE CASH

No matter where I'm traveling to, it's always important to have cash on hand. Some small shops, delis, and street vendors are cash only; plus, you don't want to be caught hunting for an ATM in an area you're unfamiliar with. This is true not only for traveling but in general. For instance, if there's an emergency like a hurricane where power outages might leave you unable to get services, you'll want cash.

If I'm going to a place with a foreign currency, I like to change some money at my bank before leaving the country (if possible). I've learned that sometimes when traveling, the currency exchange offices at the airports might be closed when you land, or you may not like their rates, or cabs may be cash only. I don't want to be caught in a stressful situation urgently trying to get cash. Being desperate means being vulnerable, so instead of putting myself in that position, I'll exchange a bit of money beforehand, even if the rate isn't favorable. I'll also travel with both my local currency and the foreign one, because you never know what can happen, and I don't want to be left stranded.

INTERNET WHILE TRAVELING

Do not connect to public Wi-Fi unless it is an absolute last resort and you've taken a few precautions. Criminals have been known to set up fake Wi-Fi hotspots and make the names look official to trick people into connecting to them. If you then log into your bank or do any shopping or pretty much anything on your device, the criminal will be able to see that, unless you're sticking to secure websites (with "https" in the URL), but even then, I'd rather avoid connecting to a risky situation. Even if you're using a VPN, if you're connected to a malicious network, there's still a risk. That said, a VPN does block certain hacker attacks from gaining access to your device, so it's definitely safer to connect to a public network with a VPN than without one. Plus, since most people don't use VPNs, the hacker might move on to an easier target. But I still don't like the idea of exposing myself to the risk that comes with public Wi-Fi. Instead, I pay the extra fees to use the internet from my smartphone, and if I need to connect another device, I'll use my phone as a hotspot. If I'm connecting to the internet at my hotel, I call the front desk to make sure I have the correct network name and password, but I still won't log into anything sensitive. I'll use hotel Wi-Fi to browse for the news or hot places to visit, and even so, I do it with my VPN enabled.

As a reminder, if you are shopping for a VPN, do not use the free ones. They are not as secure as other services. Instead, choose trusted brands with strong encryption and wide coverage. Look for a company that doesn't log your activity, and read up on security-driven customer reviews.

Charging your phone in public: In addition to the dangers of using public Wi-Fi, charging your phone publicly at an airport or hotel also comes with risks. The port you use to charge your device is also the same port used to transfer data, so if your phone is connected to a USB charging port, a hacker can gain access to it, and if done properly, you wouldn't even know. To protect yourself, get a USB data blocker or a USB condom (seriously—that's what they're called). They're very inexpensive and will prevent your phone from getting hacked, because it blocks data from flowing into your device so a cybercriminal can't install or execute a malicious attack. It does that while charging your phone as it normally would, and you can even get data blockers that are optimized to charge your Android or Apple device more efficiently.

As an alternative to a USB data blocker, you can plug your device directly into an AC power outlet instead of a USB charging port, and that will also keep you protected. Or you can use a portable charging bank. I love traveling with my portable charging bank, not just to keep my phone charged but to keep all my items at 100 percent battery (more on this later in this chapter).

Safety apps: (Note: Apps change frequently, so while the ones I mention may no longer be around, it's likely that similar or better apps have been developed.) When traveling, technology is always helpful: you can download a translator app—an app that can translate text to your native language—and, of course, map apps, but there are a variety of apps that are focused specifically on helping us stay safe while we travel. One of these apps, Smart Traveler, was created by the US Department of State, and it will inform you of any current travel warnings or alerts. The Centers for Disease Control also has an app where you can access news pertaining to outbreaks, travel notices, and other general information. It also has a checklist that will help you keep track of any recommended travel vaccines, and it provides you with a place to store travel and medical documents (side note: your phone may also have a health app for travel medical information).

Another safety app is called Sitata. It's an app in which you can plan and manage your trip itinerary. The app will inform you about any health, safety, or flight issues specific to your plans. It will also keep you up-to-date on anything that could delay your travel—like a transit strike—and you can use the app to share your location with friends and family so it will notify them when you've landed or arrived at your hotel. The best part of this app is that if you have a medical emergency, the Sitata app can also connect you with doctors, direct you to nearby hospitals, find emergency phone numbers, and more. There are also a variety of SOS safety apps. Some work with wearable devices such as invisaWear, Silent Beacon, or Flare, which I've previously mentioned in this book, but not all of them work internationally, and they may not work in every country, so it's good to know of other options.

bSafe is an alternative app and is available in 125 countries. The app includes an SOS alarm, which is voice or touch activated. That's a common feature, but what's unique about bSafe is its live-streaming feature, which will notify your emergency contacts (called "guardians") of your location, will let them track you, and will let them see and hear everything that's happening remotely. Your phone will also record audio and video, which will be texted to your emergency contact's phone. It can fake calls if you need a quick exit out of a situation, and you can have loved ones follow you home with the live tracking feature. Remember, with Android and Apple devices, you can also set up some of your own safety features via Apple's Shortcuts app or Google Assistant.

The American Red Cross has an Emergency app that alerts you to incoming natural disasters, and it gives you preparation tips. If you're traveling to an area (or live in an area) that's known for earthquakes, tsunamis, wildfires, or hurricanes, you may want to have this app handy. It will also tell you where nearby shelters are if needed. That said, if you are traveling to an area that's known for these natural disasters, it's best to plan around the dangerous seasons if possible. Similarly, the American Red Cross has two additional beneficial apps, First Aid and Pet First Aid, which are helpful to have year-round on your phone, but if you're traveling, the First Aid app is particularly helpful.

GeoSure is another app that will help you understand the safety of the neighborhood you're exploring, and it aims to be hyperlocal. It will alert you about all types of safety conditions like theft, violence, and basic freedoms. The preferences within the app can also be set to show safety information for specific marginalized groups, like the LGBTQ+ community.

There are also lifestyle-specific apps. If you're a woman traveling alone and want to meet up with other female travelers, Tourlina is a women's-only travel companion app. Also, if you're a runner and like to check out new routes when traveling, look for apps that will guide you on trusted, verified routes so that you don't end up running along a dangerous path. Some of these running-specific apps may include Glympse, ROAD iD, and RunGo.

One thing to note about many of these safety apps is that they do track you as part of their functionality. You can limit what you give the app permission to do, but in order to function optimally, it will ask you for location-tracking information or other permissions. If you don't want the app running 24-7, you may need to delete and reinstall when needed or go into your settings and adjust the notifications. Also, many of these apps have free as well as paid memberships.

GETTING AROUND

As outdated as a paper map may seem, I still like to carry one around with me sometimes. If my phone runs out of power, I know I'll have a backup, but also, I don't like to take out my phone more than needed when abroad. Before exploring a new city, I'll map out restaurants or tourist spots I'd like to visit. As I'm walking around, I'll glance at the folded map (still hidden in my purse) to see if there's anything nearby I'd like to visit. Usually, I fold the map to only show the area I'm in so it's not so large. You can get free smaller maps at many hotels that are easy to manage without it basically saying, "HEY, EVERYONE—I'M A TOURIST!"

That said, I also use my phone. Instead of mapping out locations every few blocks, I'll map out where I want to visit in advance. You can drop pins in your mapping app or take screenshots and then glance at the photos on your phone as a reference point. But this does depend on the destination you're traveling to. If you're in a walkable city like Barcelona or Florence, it's easy to map out a ton of destinations you'd like to visit all within a few blocks, but if you're in the countryside, you'll likely rely more heavily on your phone. However, I would still recommend a physical map because some locations have bad cell service, and you don't want to be left stranded.

These tips are good for exploring a new city, but if you have a specific destination and you're walking straight to it with no planned stops in between, then you can plug the location into your map function, grab your earbuds, and let the app guide you with the voice navigation. Of course, you don't want to be so tuned in to your earbuds that you don't know what's going on around you; having one earbud in your ear will allow you to hear the directions and pay attention to your surroundings.

CONFIDENCE IS KEY

Appearing confident protects us in many situations, and traveling is no exception. When you project confidence, you're less likely to become a victim of a street hustler, scammer, or worse. To project confidence, be decisive in your actions. This may take a bit of planning if you have to map out locations, but do your best to look like you know where you're going. Also, don't look worried, as that'll make you stick out like a sore thumb. You don't have to be cheery, but wear a gentle, calm look (the kind of facial expression you might make while scrolling through your TikTok feed). Also, your body language should appear confident as well. Stand strong, head up, walk smoothly, make eye contact, and take up space. It'll feel powerful, but it's also important that it feel natural. If it feels unnatural, then try practicing at home before your trip. Start with small challenges like walking into a restaurant or bar confidently, and then work your way up to how you stand in cocktail party–like or networking conversations. It's an important skill, whether you're interested in safety or not.

Additionally, watch how you speak; do you default to a questioning tone? A questioning tone is when your voice rises at the end of a sentence as if you were asking a question. If you have a question, that's fine, but if you're making a statement like "No, I'm not interested," you shouldn't sound like you're asking a question. Issue a definitive no, both verbally and nonverbally. Make it so that even though your words might be saying no, your body language isn't communicating, "Keep pushing—maybe you'll convince me." Be firm and don't back down.

BE ALERT

Looking alert is part of projecting confidence, but being alert means taking notice of what's around you. There are a variety of situations you may want to pay attention to—for example, when a person you don't know is walking way too close, or when there's someone who keeps popping up everywhere you go, making eye contact. Your senses would likely perk up with those scenarios, but I'm also always cautious of people on bicycles or motorcycles. Often, I notice them in groups of two or three, and they ride their bikes with speed or kind of meander like they're looking for a target. It's very different from your local food delivery guy—these cyclists don't have a destination, they're not on the traditional bike paths, and they're kind of wandering.

From my extensive traveling, I know that these bikers frequently target public plazas, particularly corners and crosswalks where it's easy to quickly grab something and take off. The bicycle or motorcycle makes for the perfect getaway, because a victim can't catch them on foot and it's nimble enough to maneuver in and out of narrow streets or traffic. When I see this kind of behavior, I keep a good grip on my purse or make sure my backpack is secured on both shoulders. If I'm standing at a street corner, I'll also hold my purse or backpack on my side farthest from the street, and I don't stand too close to the edge of the sidewalk. These types of thieves usually target people who have easy-to-grab valuables, like a camera hanging on their arm or a phone they're talking into while not paying attention to what's around them. If I feel like they're still following me, despite having made my valuables difficult to snatch, then I head into a safer public place to kill some time. I prefer hotels with a restaurant or bar where I can sit for a few hours.

While I learned to look out for bicycles and motorcycles while traveling, this isn't exclusive to international travel. I've seen this happen in my old New York neighborhood, so it's a good habit to keep your valuables close and overall be aware of what's happening around you.

DON'T GET LIT

I know, I know . . . you're trying to have fun and you want to drink. I get it, but unless you have a crew of trusted comrades who are taking charge of you for the night, I'm going to be the Mom Friend of your group and remind you that being drunk makes you a target. Even at a bar back home, it's risky, but when you're traveling, it's even more so. First, you want to get familiar with the customs. In some places, it's not only frowned upon but also illegal to be messily drunk in public. In addition, when you're traveling in a new place, you're already unfamiliar with the area and you may not even speak the local language well, so drinking heavily isn't a good idea.

I once had a horrifying experience because I was drunk. I was out at a bar, and after it closed, a friend got me a cab to go back home. It was a thirty-five-minute ride, and as I began falling asleep in the back of the car, I noticed the cab starting to turn in the wrong direction. I was drunk but conscious, and I knew my way home. In that moment of fear, I suddenly perked up and started paying attention to what was around me. I immediately told the driver to turn in the direction of where I wanted to go. As I spoke to him, I checked my door to make sure the window rolled down and the child locks weren't on. I left the window rolled down until he got close enough to my apartment that I felt safe walking home. Then I told him to leave me on the corner and I jumped out. I stood outside a random apartment building, fumbling around in my purse, and when he drove off, I walked to my actual apartment. That was the last time I let my guard down while drinking. In a group of friends who are headed back home together, drinking heavily certainly feels safer, but when I drink, I still like to maintain my ability to make lucid decisions. That's a personal preference. If you're trying to get totally wasted, at least make sure you have a Mom Friend nearby who's looking out for you, a role I've played many times. (I may or may not have been referred to as the "hawk" by a few men at bars for not letting my girls out of sight.)

KNOW KEY PHRASES

If you're traveling to a country where you don't speak the language, learn some key phrases to help you get around. The basics—*please*, *thank you*, *yes*, and *no*—are musts, but also learn how to say, "I don't speak the language," "Where is the bathroom?" "Where's the exit?" and "I need help." Also learn how to read words like *exit*, because it will help you identify emergency exits; plus, when taking public transit, the stations usually have the exit signs written in their local language.

ASK FOR HELP

Don't be afraid to ask for help. Approaching strangers when we're traveling can be scary. After all, what if you pick a criminal to help you? You might take comfort in knowing that's unlikely. Usually, the criminal will pick you. They'll offer you unsolicited advice or help, so if someone approaches you randomly offering assistance, that should raise a red flag, but if you ask for help, you'll likely choose a nonthreatening person. That said, exercise caution. If you're asking for directions, you can go into a restaurant or store to ask an employee. If you're asking someone to take a photo, look for a family who might be taking photos nearby or a group of friends. And in an emergency, don't hesitate to ask for help, because chances are you'll pick someone who is just a regular person willing to assist you.

STOP YOUR MAIL

When you're away from work, you probably set up an out-of-office reply, but what about the physical mail that gets delivered to your home? In the United States, the postal service allows you to request a "hold mail" service, and you can do this online, by phone, or in person at your local post office. You can request this up to thirty days in advance. I recommend putting the request in at least a week before you leave and adding a few days to account for any errors. The post office should stop your mail immediately, but in my experience mistakes have happened, so I pad my dates.

Whether or not you request that the post office hold your mail depends on the length of your travels. If you're only going away for the weekend, you don't need to hold your mail, but if you're going away for two weeks, then you should request that your mail be put on hold. If you're going away for a longer period—for example, renting a home for the summer—then request that your mail be forwarded, but still add the shoulder dates just in case. Also, the more time you give the post office to fulfill your request, the less likely you'll have mail accidentally delivered.

That said, if you have someone you trust to check on your mail, that would be ideal. You can still put in the hold-mail or forwarding request, but ask a neighbor to check as well so they can pick up any mail that was delivered accidentally or pick up things that may not go through the post office, like a local newspaper.

Remember that having your mail pile up in a mailbox is a sign to criminals that the home is empty and can be an invitation for theft. In my neighborhood, there was a family who had gone on vacation for about two weeks. They didn't have cameras or an alarm system, and when they came back from vacation, they learned their home had been burglarized. It had been days since the burglary happened, so there were no leads, neighbors couldn't recall anything suspicious, and police filed a report but there were no suspects.

I recommend having an alarm system and cameras in place, but also don't advertise that you're away by letting mail pile up in the mailbox. Also, identity theft is a very real issue, and thieves who specialize in that type of crime can steal right out of the mailbox. I've had three pieces of mail stolen with highly sensitive information, and they were never returned. If that ever happens to you, there are steps you can take to mitigate the damage, such as paying for identity theft monitoring services or freezing your credit. But prevention is always the best tactic, so if you can forward mail, put a hold on it, or ask a neighbor or family member to help while you're away, that should be your first line of defense. And as a thank-you, when you get back from your trip, you can bring them a nice souvenir.

FOOD SAFETY

There's nothing worse than being on a beautiful vacation and getting food poisoning. Depending on where you're traveling to, look up what you can and cannot eat ahead of time. In many countries, the tap water is not safe to drink, so foods that are washed with that water, like salads or fruits, are also not safe to eat. If the tap water is unsafe, opt for bottled drinks, or use a reusable water bottle that you can fill with purified water. Avoid drinks with ice made from tap water, and if you're given a wet glass, remember that it was probably washed with tap water. This also applies while brushing your teeth or showering: don't let the tap water get into your mouth, and always brush with purified water. I personally like to pack an extra toothbrush when I'm traveling to countries where I can't drink the tap in case I mess up and contaminate my toothbrush.

Avoid fruits you can't peel, not only because they're likely washed in the contaminated water but also because you can't be sure what fertilizers or pesticides were used in producing that food. For example, in Ecuador, strawberries could contain a parasitic worm that causes trichinosis due to fertilizers that are made from pig fecal matter. You can eat them if they're washed very well, but if you're not sure or aren't able to wash them well yourself, it's better to avoid fruits you can't peel. When it comes to cleaning food, you may come across people suggesting a bleach-and-water dilution to sanitize food, but if the ratios aren't correct, you can end up poisoning yourself or damaging your internal tissues, since bleach is corrosive. I personally avoid bleach near any food surfaces (even the kitchen counter). Instead, I'll use a vinegar-and-salt dilution, which is much safer, as you can soak your fruits or veggies in that to clean them.

Generally, foods that are safe to eat when traveling include those that are served steaming hot, or dry, canned, and packaged foods. Still, it's not a guarantee that you won't get sick. In Thailand I had a great vacation until my last night, when our tour group shared a good-bye dinner. The next day, at least four or five of us got sick, including me. (This is especially not fun when you have a twenty-four-hour flight home with layovers.) I was stocked with activated charcoal pills (a hack I learned in my first aid class), and while it wasn't instant relief, it did help me recover enough that I wasn't miserable the entire trip home.

Additionally, be extra careful with street food. I won't judge—I'm an adventurous eater—but when I'm traveling, I try to avoid street vendors. When I do eat from street vendors, I look for ones that are popular and that look very clean. I also avoid anything exotic to my palate, like insects or fish eyeballs. In Thailand, two people in my group ate eyeballs and both got sick and ended up missing two days of the trip while they recovered in a hotel. I'm all for adventure, but exercise caution when deciding what adventure is worth it and what's not.

TRAVEL INSURANCE

Whether or not you choose to purchase travel insurance will depend on your budget, the destination you're traveling to, your health insurance plan, and any credit card perks you may have. Travel insurance focuses on two aspects of your trip: your reservations and any medical expenses that may arise while traveling. How much is covered will depend on the type of plan you book. There are certain occasions where it's certainly best to book it.

If you've prepaid for an expensive international trip where you cannot cancel, travel insurance is probably a good idea. If you're traveling to a location with high-risk weather or to a place where injury or sickness are more possible than usual, travel insurance likely might be necessary. Hiking in Machu Picchu sounds fabulous (personally, I took the train—no hiking for me—but for those adventure lovers, it sounds great); however, if something goes wrong, it's not easy to get medical attention and those costs can rack up quickly. In this instance, I'd recommend a comprehensive travel insurance plan. The same could apply to cruises where you're paying up front. Check with the company policies to see what kind of vacation protection they offer and if there are additional packages you can purchase. With that said, if you're traveling domestically or taking a road trip, you probably don't need travel insurance. There is some financial risk with those trips as well, but it's not as hefty as traveling abroad and booking a cruise or a tour. The bottom line is that if the financial risk is low and you can afford to lose any prepaid expenses, you can skip the travel insurance. Further, it's likely you can use your health insurance should something come up while you're traveling.

Keep in mind there are a variety of travel insurance plans, so the extent of coverage you need will depend on whether your health insurance is accepted abroad and what kind of credit card perks you may have. Many health insurance plans will cover customary and reasonable hospital costs, but a medical evacuation is a completely different story. Also, there are credit cards that offer travel protections such as lost-baggage reimbursement and car rental protection, and some even offer trip cancellation or interruption protection, so make sure to explore these options when booking a trip.

POSTING ON SOCIAL MEDIA

If you're active on social media, you're going to hate this tip (I do, and I'm the one giving it to you). Pretty much every safety-inclined person, from experts to bloggers, will tell you not to post while you're on vacation. The risk is that someone will use that information to target your home for burglaries. Similarly, if you post what you're doing in the moment, that could expose you to other personal safety risks. Kim Kardashian's 2016 robbery in Paris is a good example of this. Career criminals used her social media to know when she was arriving in France and what jewelry she had on her, which helped them plan their attack. We don't all get the attention that Kim K. gets, but still, it's a reminder that posting in the moment has its risks.

While at home, I personally like posting once I've left a location. I'll take videos or photos in the moment and store them until I'm at the next location. When it comes to posting that I'm on vacation, however, this is much harder to avoid. If you're active on social, there's an expectation that you'll post, since social media is supposed to feel like it's in the moment and real. But the truth of the matter is that sometimes it is, sometimes it isn't. You can certainly plan posts or take photos of things that aren't obviously vacation photos, but you can also take a few other steps to mitigate your risks.

You can have a house sitter monitor your house; you can tell your trusted neighbors you'll be away, so they'll notice any suspicious activity. My favorite option is to use smart cameras as well as alarm systems. With a smart alarm system and cameras, you can see if a window or door has been opened right from your phone. Your alarm system will alert you through its app; plus, you'll have eyes and ears with the cameras. The only downside is that if there's a power outage, you'll lose connectivity. But this is where neighbors again can be helpful. You can even use keyless entry devices or smart garage door openers to give a trusted friend access to your home in an emergency without having to give them your main access code or a physical key. And with a smart alarm system, you can turn the alarm on and off remotely.

There's still a risk when you post on social media that you're on vacation, but having these extra steps in place helps me feel like I can still enjoy social media while being cautious.

TRAVEL PERKS

All right—this one isn't necessarily safety related, but it will make your vacations easier if you have a long layover. A lot of credit cards offer entrances to VIP airport lounges where you get access to free food, Wi-Fi, lounging chairs, and private bathrooms, some of which have showers. Before leaving on your trip, check with your bank and credit cards to see if you have any of these perks available at the airports you'll be traveling to. If your credit cards don't offer this perk and you have a long layover at an airport, then you can see if there's a VIP lounge that offers day passes. Some airports also have pod hotels where you can rest during a long layover (for a small fee). I used that while in Russia. It wasn't luxurious, but I couldn't leave the airport without a visa and needed a place to rest.

WHAT TO PACK

If there's anything I've learned in all my travels, it is that you must prepare for every scenario. At some point, your luggage may get lost, your plane may get delayed overnight, your airplane may be too small to stash your carry-on, or you may forget that you can't brush with the tap and now you've contaminated your toothbrush. Do these all seem wildly specific? That's because all of these instances—and a few more—have happened to me, so I've learned to pack accordingly. Here's a list of things I pack on most trips, and it's mainly items I keep in my carry-on:

✓ **Electronics:** These must go in your carry-on, and it's best to limit what you take on a trip. If you can rely on your phone and a tablet for entertainment, do that. Try not to bring your entire office with you, because if you lose it while traveling, that's not fun. Basically, if you can't afford to lose it, leave it at home and make sure everything is backed up before you travel.

✓ **A reusable tote:** These are a must for shopping or carrying drinks and snacks while you explore, but I've also been on several flights where the plane was so small I had to take out valuables from my carry-on and transfer them to a plastic bag the airlines gave me. The bags are barely large enough to carry some snacks and a water bottle, so I've learned to just bring my own tote. If I am asked to check my carry-on luggage, I know I have a tote large enough to take out the essentials (bonus if you find one with a zipper—and make sure it has comfortable handles).

✓ **A change of clothes:** If you're traveling with a checked bag and your flight gets delayed or your luggage gets lost, you'll be grateful to have packed a change of clothes in your carry-on. I keep it simple and lightweight: yoga pants, shorts, T-shirts, and undergarments. All of these items are small, so it still leaves a lot of room in my carry-on for other items. I also like to pack enough for two days so that gives me time to have the airport find my luggage and/or buy more clothes if my checked bags ever get lost. And don't forget your sunglasses!

✓ **A sweater or poncho:** I think every grandma in human history has warned of the dangers of a cold breeze. And when it comes to the airport, every grandma was right. When I travel, it feels like a constant battle between hot and cold, so I always plan to dress in layers. Plus, if you have layovers in countries with a dress code, you'll want a quick way to cover up. I like to carry a lightweight sweater or poncho, and I'll layer a tank underneath in case it gets unbearably hot. That said, I've had layovers in places like Dubai or Qatar where I simply was not comfortable walking around in a tank even though it was hot, so I covered up to be respectful of the local norms.

✓ **Travel adaptors:** If I'm traveling to a country with different outlets, I always pack a travel adaptor in my carry-on because there's no way I'm going to risk a dead battery on my phone or tablet if my luggage gets lost. I'll travel with a few adaptors, and I'll put the extras in my checked luggage, but at least one will go in my carry-on with me.

✓ **Toiletries and makeup:** Whether you're on a long flight where you'll want to freshen up or preparing in case your checked bag gets lost, pack a travel toothbrush, toothpaste, deodorant, feminine products, mouth rinse, facial cleanser, wipes, lip balm, hand sanitizer, hair tie, lotion, tissues, and a hairbrush. (Just be sure that all liquids, gels, and pastes are in containers of 3.4 ounces or less, and that they can all fit inside one quart-size resealable bag.) I also like to have my makeup and skincare items with me, mainly because I don't want them to break if my luggage is tossed around. Long flights also tend to dry out my skin, so my disposable sheet masks and lotion come in handy. Your travel buddy might be a little embarrassed by the sheet masks, but your skin will thank you for it. Plus, what else are you going to do on an eighteen-hour flight? Speaking of which, on long flights, dry shampoo is helpful to carry as well, especially if you have hair that gets greasy quickly.

✓ **Documents and medications:** This one seems self-explanatory, but any important travel documents like itineraries, your passport copies, transportation information, and agency phone numbers must come on board with you so you're not caught scrambling if your luggage gets lost. If you use any daily medications, contact lenses and solution, or vitamins, bring those as well. I also like to pack some first aid medicines. I bring activated charcoal pills in case of an upset stomach (these really helped when I got food poisoning abroad), pain relievers for headaches, and depending on where I'm traveling to, I'll bring allergy medicine or some motion sickness medications. When traveling abroad, the medication names are different, and sometimes they're sold in packs, but in some places, you buy single pills. Keep in mind, particularly if there are language barriers, it can be tough to navigate finding the right medication when abroad, so I always pack the basics with me.

✓ **Phone charger and backup battery pack:** Portable battery packs can only be packed in carry-on luggage. Whether you're checking in for a flight via a kiosk or with an agent, they usually ask to make sure you haven't packed them in your luggage, giving you a chance to take them out. If they don't ask or you forget, it will probably be removed from your bag and the airport will toss it, so check your airline's policies ahead of time if you have any questions. Either way, be prepared to take this on board with you.

✓ **Valuables:** Don't tempt the luggage screeners by putting your expensive jewelry, camera, or other luxury items in your checked bags. I prefer to leave most of my valuables at home, but whatever important items you're traveling with, make sure you bring them in your carry-on bag. This includes any expensive clothes as well. If you have anything you've splurged on that's important to you, put it in your carry-on bag.

✓ **Zip ties:** I like to pack a few mini zip ties in my carry-on in case I need to use one as a luggage lock. I'll also pack a pair of small nail scissors and put it in the outside zippered pocket so I can quickly untie my bag. Keep in mind there are limitations on the sharp objects you can pack in a carry-on, but if it's a small pair of scissors (less than four inches in length, according to the Transportation Security Administration), that's usually allowed on board. You can put a backup in an outside zippered pocket of your checked bag as well just in case the screening agent takes them.

✓ **A water bottle and snacks:** There are tons of reasons to travel with your own reusable water bottle. Waste prevention and sustainability are certainly two of them, but it'll also save you a fortune in water purchases. And depending on where you're traveling, water may be harder to come by, so you'll want to make sure you're prepared. Remember that water bottles have to be empty until you've passed through TSA's security screenings, and you'll also have to be mindful of water safety. If you can't drink the tap water, then you won't want to refill the bottle at any water station unless you know it's been purified. For example, in Thailand I couldn't drink from the tap, but every hotel I went to would refill my water bottle. Snacks are also a must. I like to pack salty snacks, sweets, a source of protein, and granola bars. I also pack enough to last most of the trip. There are so many times when I've been stuck in an airport when all the shops are closed or I've been in my hotel with late-night cravings (I'm a chocoholic), wishing I had a snack to munch on. Now I always travel with my own snacks, and if I can, I buy more as I go along. Keep in mind that you can only carry wrapped, nonliquid snacks. So, you can bring your own sandwich, yogurt, and fruit, but you can't bring soup on a plane.

✓ **Entertainment:** I like to bring magazines I can leave behind when I'm done with them or a book that will last the trip, and, of course, I download a ton of shows on my tablet. If it's a short trip, I don't need anything other than my phone, but if it's a fourteen-hour flight, for instance, I use that time to binge all my favorite shows. And don't forget your headphones with adaptors. Remember

that not every airplane has the standard headphone jack we're used to, so if you're using noise-cancelling wired headphones, you might need an adaptor. Also keep in mind that wireless headphones won't work with the TVs on planes, so you might want to bring wired headphones. On longer flights, attendants usually hand out headphones as well, so you can use those in a pinch.

✓ **Compression socks:** If you're on a long flight, consider bringing compression socks to help with circulation. These will keep your feet from falling asleep and prevent swelling by slightly squeezing your legs to help the veins and muscles move blood more efficiently. To help with circulation, you can also walk around on the flight, stretch in your seat, and of course, stay hydrated.

✓ **Comfort items:** Bring items like your travel pillow, travel socks, ear plugs, or eye masks—really, anything that helps you feel comfortable on a flight—on board with you. It can be hard resting on a plane with all the commotion and noise happening around you, but if there are items that can help you feel comfortable, don't hesitate to bring them in your carry-on.

✓ **Cleaning supplies:** I'm a bit of a germaphobe, so while I always have hand sanitizer on me, I also like to carry a mini aerosol cleaning spray and antibacterial wipes when I travel. Keep in mind that when you're traveling abroad, some countries don't let you pack aerosols on board, so you may want to check ahead of time or be prepared for it to be taken away.

✓ **Pen and paper:** The paper is optional but helpful if you need to take notes, like reminders of places you want to check out when you land. The pen, though, is an absolute must. When you're filling out a customs form on international flights, you're lucky if you're handed a pen; usually you're told there are pens at the gate or you're given these tiny pencils with dull points and loads of germs. *Nope.* I'll stick to my own pen, thank you. Plus, it comes in handy in loads of other places as well: splitting a check at a restaurant, crossword puzzles, whatever the need.

✓ **A mini sewing kit:** This doesn't necessarily go in my carry-on, but I always travel with a mini sewing kit. You never know when you might lose a button. I'm not skilled with a needle but I can do the basics, and as a Mom Friend, this has come in handy for me. Once, on a ferry from mainland Spain to Ibiza, a guy in my tour group had his pants button pop off. He was embarrassed and traveled light, so he really needed those pants. Out of twenty-six of us in the group, I was the only one with a mini sewing kit. Mom Friend to the rescue!

✓ **Mini first aid kit:** Aside from the medication basics I already mentioned, don't forget to pack items to deal with shoe blisters and cuts. I'll pack bandages in my carry-on with some antiseptic and alcohol wipes, while any extra items can go in my checked bag. You can find premade packs online, and sometimes you get them for free as promotional materials from companies. I'll keep those freebies in my car or save them for trips when I need a mini first aid kit.

✓ **Rain gear:** If you have the room, grab a mini umbrella or poncho and throw it in your carry-on. This is another lesson I learned the hard way. When you travel, you hope for the best weather, but when your expected sunny and clear days turn to three days of rainfall, you'll be glad you brought an umbrella. Worst-case scenario, you can probably buy one on your trip, but this again may depend on where you're traveling to. In some countries, it's difficult to come across items that you might consider basics.

✓ **General packing thoughts:** When I pack my carry-on, I like to think about what I'm going to access the most, and I layer the items accordingly. My emergency change of clothes will be at the bottom of the bag, while my entertainment and snacks are at the top. I know that as I go through security checks, I'll have to take out electronics and any liquids, creams, or aerosols for screening, so I keep them accessible. Once I'm headed on board, I'll want those items again, and if they're on top I can quickly grab them so I can get settled in my seat without holding up the line or having to open my entire suitcase.

And I know that I mentioned this earlier, but it's important enough to reiterate: Make sure you do your research and see if there are items that you consider to be basics that are difficult to find abroad. For example, when I go to Cuba, I always bring a ton of hand sanitizer, wipes, and toilet paper. The hotels will have toilet paper, but when you're touring, the bars and restaurants rarely have toilet paper or soap in the bathrooms. On my first trip to Cuba, I went to a ton of stores looking to buy toilet paper and couldn't find it anywhere—I was with locals, too, and still had no luck. My hotel had some, so I wasn't desperate, but for any trip afterward, I made sure to pack extra. If you're not sure what to expect in the country you're traveling to, maybe pack a few travel tissue packs that can double as toilet paper in a pinch.

ACCOMMODATIONS

This is a big one! Let me start by saying that I worked in hotels for nearly a decade. (I started when I was a teen.) I worked the front desk and in housekeeping, food service, and ultimately sales. I've also traveled a ton both for work and personally, so, all in all, I've easily stayed in more than one hundred hotels. Given that I talk about safety nearly every day, a common topic I encounter is hotel safety, and in my experience, there are two issues that I've seen countless times firsthand. These include theft resulting from guests leaving luggage unattended in the lobby and theft resulting from guests forgetting to close their safes and people unexpectedly walking into their rooms. The latter could be housekeeping, who usually knock first, but sometimes the front desk accidentally assigns two guests to the same room, so another guest may walk in on you. I've probably done this as an inexperienced front desk agent myself, and it's happened to me a few times while traveling. It's never been threatening in my experience, just a simple computer error, but if I weren't in the habit of locking my hotel door, it could've been creepy.

I have always felt safe while traveling and staying in hotels, meaning that my biggest concern has been theft, because when you're traveling with limited items, everything is valuable. Hotels generally take theft very seriously, and if they're tech savvy, it's easy to catch the thief, but for the traveling victim, catching a thief several days after—which is usually how long it takes for room records and video files to be reviewed—isn't helpful. You want your stuff back immediately, and that's unlikely to happen.

Even with my hospitality work experience, I still don't like to tempt fate by leaving valuables unattended and out in the open. What's considered "valuable" may vary based on where I'm traveling to, and that's something I take into consideration when packing.

Here are a few things to take into account when thinking about your accommodations and safety:

- **Arriving safely:** When booking your flights and accommodations, seek to arrive during normal business operating hours. After hours, hotels have limited staff and they may lock the front doors for their own safety, in which case, if the staff happens to be away from the phone or the bell, you might be stuck outside your hotel for a while. This is also true with Airbnbs and other vacation homes. Plan to arrive during the day, and if you are delayed, communicate that with the people who are expecting you.

- **Transportation:** Some hotels offer free airport transfers and others do not. Find out what your hotel offers ahead of time and the hours of operation for it. Alternatively, prebook a taxi to come pick you up. This again depends on the place you're visiting: New York City has taxis 24-7 at airports, but an island like Santorini in Greece does not. When I was in Santorini, there were a total of about thirty taxis on the island (no app-based taxi services either), and although I had prebooked transport from the port to my hotel, there was a line of tourists waiting for available transportation. I had something similar happen in a remote part of Italy where one cab would pass every twenty minutes or so, and there was no official line or place to get help. You simply waited and hoped you were in the right place. Do your research ahead of time and avoid doing this at night.

- **Selecting your accommodations:** This is the most important step for traveling safely. Don't compromise your safety or comfort for a lower price. Stick to hotels that are well rated, and while that usually comes with a bit of a price increase, it's worth every penny. It doesn't have to be a five-star hotel (I wish!), but I like to stick to hotels that are three stars and above. I look for hotels that look clean, have good online reviews, are staffed round-the-clock, and are in a safer neighborhood. Personally, I stay away from hotels where I'm sharing a room or bathroom with strangers. I know all those college road trip movies make it look like a blast, but as a female traveler, I simply don't feel safe under those circumstances.

- **Reserving a room:** When you reserve a room, request that it be above the ground floor. It's said that the safest floors are between the third and sixth floors, because the lower floors are easier to break into, and in the case of a fire, a fire truck ladder is about seventy-five to one hundred feet in length, so it can easily reach the sixth floor of a building. Maybe a fire isn't your greatest concern when traveling, but if your ground floor window faces an open parking lot, it can be uncomfortable. Sometimes you don't have a choice, as a hotel may only have one or two floors, but this is where doing your research ahead of time may come in handy. Maybe there's another hotel nearby, and if there isn't, then that's when knowing there's 24-7 security and good lighting will help you feel more comfortable.

    This is also the time to request any other room preferences, such as being near an elevator or near the front of the hotel. Know that requests aren't guaranteed, but if it's in your reservation notes, it will help the hotel staff sort out the rooms.

- **Checking in:** You've arrived and now it's time to get settled in. Hopefully you've arrived during the day when the hotel is fully staffed and better equipped to take care of any issues that might come up, like switching your room if something's broken. Plus, daylight will help you identify any threats, particularly if you're traveling by yourself.

    Before checking in, consider downloading the hotel app if they have one (do this before you arrive). It can speed up the check-in process, earn you rewards points, and sometimes hotels give away some freebies just for downloading the app, like a waived resort fee or Wi-Fi charge, breakfast, even room upgrades. Plus, the apps usually have important information like a directory or hotel map. As with all apps, check the privacy policy before downloading and adjust any default settings.

We Mom Friends love freebies, but back to the safety stuff. If you're checking in at a front desk, keep your bags close. Do not leave them unattended in some corner of the lobby. Remember that anyone can walk in and out of a lobby and grab something from your bag. When I worked at a hotel in Miami, a guest's passport was stolen from her bag in the middle of a packed lobby during breakfast. There were people all around, it was an open floor plan, and not a single person, including me, noticed the thief walk in and steal the passport. I learned an important lesson that day: no matter how nice the hotel is, no matter how safe and comfy it feels, keep your valuables close. Now when I travel, my purse comes with me always, even to the omelet station—I'm not taking any chances.

Also, front desk employees should be trained not to say your room number out loud. They typically write it on an envelope with your room key (some hotels also use their apps for keyless entry). That said, they may say it out loud or give you elevator directions, which may give away where your room is. If there are people around who could have heard, you can ask to have your room changed. It's also best to be proactive and quietly remind them that with a full lobby, you want to make sure you can maintain your privacy while checking in. The proactive measure is the best call here, because if the hotel is sold out, they may not be able to change your room, and that could leave you feeling uncomfortable. If you proactively let the front desk know privacy is important to you, they can take the proper precautions.

You can also let the staff know that you're not expecting any guests so not to let any calls or guests through, and you can even place the room under a pseudonym. Celebrities do that all the time when they're trying to avoid the fan frenzy. Of course, we're not all celebrities with tons of fans hoping to catch a glimpse, but there are times when we may want to borrow from the "celebrity book of safety."

Also, while at the front desk, make sure you get the correct Wi-Fi information—remember that connecting to public Wi-Fi is always a risk, but one way to prevent connecting to a malicious network is to verify the correct network name and password while checking in. You'll also want to grab a business card or two when you're at the front desk. This way, if your phone battery dies, you can hand the business card to a taxicab driver to get back to your hotel. Always keep this business card on you.

I also like to ask for two keys when I check in. I do this in case I lose one or a card becomes deactivated by my phone or credit cards, but some people say they do this for safety reasons as well. If you don't want the front desk to know you're a solo traveler, ask for two keys. While I don't think that it's the most effective safety measure you can take, I've always asked for two keys for convenience. And if you do lose a key, ask the hotel to reset the key and issue you new ones. It only takes a few moments, and if anyone lifted the key from you, it'll stop them from being able to get into your room.

- **Upon getting to your room:** Do a quick inspection of the bed, closets, and curtains. It's a good habit to have for safety reasons, especially if you're traveling with children or pets, in which case you'll want to make sure there are no choking hazards, sharp objects, or medications left behind that they can get into. Also, make sure that your windows and doors lock, and check to make sure everything else is working properly as well, meaning that the toilet flushes, the water in the shower drains, and the AC works. Unless you're in a five-star hotel, the service technicians at hotels are not 24-7, so if you discover problems after hours, you'll have to wait until the next day to get service. If you check everything the second you get to your room, you can get your issue serviced faster or at least have your room changed (assuming the hotel isn't sold out). Also, become familiar with the nearby emergency exits (this is true of any establishment). How far away are the emergency exits from your room? If the hallway was full of smoke, would you be able to find them? What about in the lobby? Some travelers run drills, but even taking brief notice will help you feel that much more prepared should an emergency come up.

- **In your room:** Whenever you're in your room, lock the doors. This is a recurring theme throughout this book, and it's because it's so important. Do not rely on the door to shut on its own behind you. Make sure it's closed, locked, and if there's a dead bolt, use it. If you get a knock at your door, even if they're claiming to be a hotel employee, don't open the door if you're not expecting anyone. If you ordered extra towels and shortly after someone comes to your door from the hotel, it's probably your extra towels. To be sure, you can open the door with the security chain engaged, then disengage it and get your towels or room service or whatever else you may have requested. If you didn't order anything, then don't open the door even with the security chain engaged; instead, call the front desk and ask them if they've sent anyone to your room.

- **Safety tools for extra hotel security:** As I've said, I've been to a lot of hotels, and I can tell you from experience that some hotels have safes and others don't. Most have dead bolts and security chains; others do not. When you stick to a branded hotel, they usually have consistent global standards, but even that's not guaranteed, so the following is my go-to list of a few portable tools you can bring with you when you're traveling. You don't need all of them, but one or two are helpful; plus, a few of these are already in most hotel rooms.

  Portable door locks: These come in a few different options. Essentially, it's a piece of steel that's inserted into the door's strike plate, then locked in place with a handle. It can only be used on doors that are hinged and swing inward (no double doors or outward-swinging doors). If they fit on the door and aren't damaging anything, hotel, dorm, or apartment building managers won't mind. They're very easy to install too. Some people may be concerned about fire safety when using them, since they can delay a quick exit, but I personally prefer having a secured door. They're easy to disengage too.

  Portable doorstop alarms: Portable doorstop alarms are a great bonus security device. When you're in the room, you wedge the alarm under the door and turn on the alarm (it's battery operated), and if someone were to open the door, the alarm would alert you. Additionally, alarms are a big deterrent, so the screeching sound alone may scare away an intruder. This isn't exclusively for hotels—it can also be used for apartments, dorms, or even just for messing with a sibling that keeps going into your room. Another version of this is a door jammer, but it doesn't have an alarm.

Travel door alarm: This is a different version of a door alarm. Instead of the wedge design, this one is on a small lanyard. It has a pin that you place in a crack between the door (or window) and the frame, and if someone opens it, it sets off the alarm. These are small and lightweight, and people use them for travel, but they're also useful if you're on a road trip and need to sleep in your car or you're in a dorm or apartment. It's loud like the door stop alarm but slightly more versatile and a little smaller.

Portable safes: Most hotels have safes, but if they don't, you can usually put highly valuable items in a safe at the front desk. That said, the safes at the front desk are usually small, so you may not be able to fit your valuables in them, or maybe you simply don't trust the hotel's safes—whatever the reason, there are portable safes available. Most portable safes are either a small metal box with keys or a bag with a combination lock. They're easy to use, but in order to secure these safes, you have to loop the steel cable around something that can't be moved, like a pipe or a closet rod. Ideally, you'll want to keep it hidden as well to avoid any unnecessary attention—you can hide it in a bathrobe or behind some luggage. These safes are also ideal for small objects like cash, jewelry, or a passport.

Hidden camera detectors: I haven't come across these while traveling (although I did find a hidden camera in the bathroom of a boy's apartment once—more on that below), but I know it's a concern for many. To learn how to best detect hidden cameras, get familiar with what they might look like and their common hiding places. A quick online search for hidden cameras will help you find the most popular ones sold. Often, they're hidden in picture frames, phone chargers, smoke detectors, wall sockets, and even pens. The easiest way to identify them is with tools that are built specifically to detect hidden cameras. You can also look at what devices are connected to the Wi-Fi and see if you find something obvious like "camera," but this isn't the most reliable method.

For a more in-depth search, remember that cameras need power sources, so an easy place to start is by looking at spots where items can be plugged in. The easiest method I've found to identify a hidden camera is by using a red LED light tool. You'll have to get up close to see the light reflect off the back of the camera lens (it's easier if the room is dark), though, and I'd recommend practicing so you get used to what it looks like. There are some brands that will mail you a practice lens with your LED light tool so you can familiarize yourself with how it works.

But we're not done—we'll also want to see if we spot any cameras with infrared or invisible light, such as with night-vision cameras. We can't see this light with our eyes, but we can see it with some of our devices. Some cell phone cameras can work, but an alternative is a computer camera or even a digital camera. Point your camera toward the area where you suspect there might be a hidden camera and you'll see a bright flare; it looks like a spotlight. The red LED method takes some practice, but the infrared method couldn't be easier—and, of course, there are devices that specialize in this too. You might even be able to buy a combo device that has a red LED light and an infrared camera detector.

But back to the hidden camera that I found. I didn't

use any of the above methods, as I didn't suspect any hidden cameras, but nonetheless, I found one. I was showering at my boyfriend's apartment, and as I was rinsing my hair, I noticed a little red light in a soap box. I had no idea what it could be, but I opened the box to inspect it, and that's when I saw a little device. It looked like a mini remote control, and as I checked it out, I noticed a USB port. That's when I knew. I had no reason to suspect a hidden camera—I'd been in this apartment a million times and felt 100 percent comfortable there—but after realizing what it was I'd found, I was terrified. I immediately knew who planted the camera, because when I got out of the shower I ran to my boyfriend's room and heard his roommate ripping apart the bathroom. Clearly the roommate was looking for the camera, which he never found because I took it.

Bottom line: people and cameras can be sneaky, and even when you're not expecting it, your instincts might kick in to help you spot danger.

Portable security camera: If you're concerned, you can also buy your own portable security camera for your travels. As long as you're occupying the hotel room, it's allowed (you can always call to double-check), but if you accidentally leave it behind, you can get yourself in some trouble, so make sure you remove any devices you bring in with you.

Do Not Disturb sign: This is my favorite hotel feature, and I use it for a ton of reasons. In terms of safety, I'd rather not have strangers coming in and out of my room every day, and in speaking to sustainability, I don't need fresh towels every day. Even though many hotels have rules in place to reduce waste, like asking you to put towels on the floor if you want them replaced and hang them behind the door if you don't, I find that housekeep-

DO NOT DISTURB

ing will refresh them no matter where I put the towels, so I use my Do Not Disturb sign. Pro tip: If the Do Not Disturb sign has a local language, display the side with the local language.

Tissues: The peephole can be creepy, and after what happened to former ESPN anchor Erin Andrews, when a stalker placed surveillance on her through her hotel door peephole, I think we're all still recovering from the peephole trauma. One easy hack is to take a piece of tissue paper and stuff it in the door's peephole.

Hiding spots: When the hotel doesn't have a safe or your item is too big or maybe you don't trust the hotel safe, try some in-plain-sight hiding spots. You can tape things under a drawer or hide them under the cover of an ironing board. If what you're hiding is thin, you can drop it behind the emergency exit instructions on the back of your hotel door, and of course, you can always place items in a hidden portion of your luggage. When I close my luggage, I leave the zipper in a particular position so I can tell if it's been opened. I might also use my luggage wheels as an indicator that it's been moved. Whether it's in the luggage or in a drawer, or even lying on the bathroom vanity shelf, a hidden-pocket scrunchie is a good place to hide cash, or I might hide some in a hidden-pocket scarf hanging in the closet. Get creative with it.

- **Coming and going in and out of your hotel:** This tip will vary based on the hotel, but try to use the main entrance to come and go from your hotel versus any obscure side entrances, particularly at night. The main entrances are where you'll find most of the staff, and there's safety in numbers. However, some hotels lock the front doors after hours, and some properties are so spread out that it makes sense to use another entrance. Also, when you're walking around the hotel, avoid conversations that give away your itinerary. For example, if you're on the phone with a friend, don't discuss when and where you're meeting the friend as you're walking from the lobby to the elevator. It's very easy for anyone to overhear and possibly follow you. The same is true when you're chatting with cabdrivers. Often when traveling, taxicab drivers will recommend restaurants and places to visit. These tips are helpful, but they don't need to know that you'll be at their favorite bar at 8 p.m. tonight. Keep your chats friendly and vague and take all the useful tips you can get, but don't make your exact plans known.

The same is true with anyone who's chatty at the hotel. Anyone asking questions such as how long you're staying, if you're traveling alone, or if you're staying at the hotel should raise a red flag. A stranger who's just chatting it up by the coffee bar doesn't need to know that much information about your travel plans. You can politely lie or be vague, but if the person pushes, that's your signal to make a quick exit. Someone being persistent or aggressive about your responses to questions that make you uncomfortable is never a good a sign. Learn to recognize the early signs of this manipulation tactic so you can protect yourself.

On that note, when you're exploring a new city, if you feel like you're being followed (or need to use the restroom), a hotel with a lobby bar is usually a good spot to pop in. You can grab a snack or drink to kill some time and see if the person or group leaves, and if they're sticking around, the staff can help you call the police. Hotels are also a great place to be when you need to call a taxi, particularly in countries that don't have apps or have limited taxis.

- **Checking out:** Whether you're coming or going, preparation is key. Make sure you have your airport transportation figured out, all your essentials packed in your carry-on or personal item, and choose daytime departures when available. I typically don't even bother going to the front desk—I'll call from my room, tell them I'm checking out, have them email me my receipt, leave a tip for the housekeeping staff (customary in the US), and then head out.

TRAVEL MUST-HAVES

There are a ton of items you can use to help keep your valuables safe when you travel. These aren't exclusive to travel, per se, but it's probably when you'd get the most use out of them.

- **Antitheft bags:** These are an absolute must! Like any Mom Friend, I'm a huge fan of antitheft bags. These are purses or backpacks that have features that make snatch and grabs harder for thieves. Typically, antitheft bags have a slash-resistant mesh in the body of the bag and straps, which makes it harder for a thief to quickly cut the bag and steal what's inside. The bags also have locking zippers, so it's harder for a pickpocket to get in, and locking straps, so that instead of putting your purse in a shopping cart, you can loop the strap around the cart, locking your bag in place. If someone were to run and grab it, they'd take the entire shopping cart with them. Not that I recommend leaving a purse in a shopping cart, but you get the idea. The bags can also be used on wheelchairs, restaurant chairs—anywhere there are people around and you want to lock your bag in place. These bags usually also have RFID-blocking wallets built into them in case your credit cards have that technology, in which case they will block scanners from being able to read that data.

It seems with all this technology the bags might be expensive, but they're affordable, easy to find online, and unisex. They come in all kinds of styles: backpacks, crossbodies, messenger bags, fanny packs, and totes. The bags are also subtle in their design but sleek. Again, I'm a big fan!

- **Fingerprint locks:** In the chapter on home safety, we talked about keyless entry; well, there's a similar concept with travel locks, and it relies on biometrics. These biometric or fingerprint locks can be used on luggage, some backpacks, lockers—even bike locks. If you've ever lost the key to your luggage lock and had to have a hotel cut the lock off, you'll understand why a fingerprint lock is such a nice luxury. Plus, let's face it—many of us never change the default code on combination locks, so it's easy for a thief to guess the passcode. A fingerprint lock is much more secure. You can program several fingerprints to open the locks (usually five), the battery lasts up to six months, and it's rechargeable. The models that I've come across are TSA compliant, which means if a TSA agent needs to check your luggage, they can unlock it without damaging it. The ones that I own are responsive, easy to program, and have lasted me years. Sometimes if my finger position is off, it won't work, but then I simply adjust my position, and it opens right up.

- **Money belts:** This is an old-school safety item, and because of that, I think they've become less effective. A thief is aware this item exists, and while it may prevent pickpockets from getting your valuables, if you were robbed,

they'd probably ask you to lift your shirt so they can get the money belt. I also find these uncomfortable, especially if it's hot. They work for some people, but I'm not a fan.

- **Zippered wrist wallets:** I like zippered wrist wallets when I'm exercising outdoors and want to take a few items without being weighed down, but sometimes I find they can be a bit loose on my wrist, so I don't feel entirely secure with them when traveling. On a trip to Peru, my friend borrowed mine and she had $200 in the wallet. We went out for the night and at some point, the wallet slipped off without her noticing until we were headed back to the hotel. Moral of the story: if you do buy one of these, make sure it's a snug fit on your wrist.

- **Stash sandals:** You beachgoers will love this one. There are sandals that are designed with a hidden zipper pocket to slip in keys or a credit card, and some even let you store those goodies in the base of the shoe. Stash sandals are a bit harder to find in terms of brands and variety of styles, but they do exist. You can find them online, but expect limited options.

- **Pickpocket-proof clothing:** If you're not the type to walk around with a bag, scarf, or scrunchie, try pickpocket-proof clothing. They function like regular clothes but have pockets hidden throughout. There are tank top versions, polo shirts, T-shirts, shorts, and even underwear. They're a great option if you want to be completely hands-free while exploring.

- **Shoe soles:** For your closed-toed shoes, you can buy a shoe sole with storage built in. They're also unisex and can be cut down to fit the size of your shoe. While the storage bin isn't large, it's big enough to hold a key, cash, some jewelry, or medicine. If you're crafty, you can probably try making a version at home with some of your existing shoe soles.

- **Diversion wallets:** There are a few ways to approach this method. Some people travel with a wallet that has nothing but a few dollars inside in case it gets stolen; in my case, I split up my cash, credit cards, and IDs so that if my wallet is stolen, I'm not completely devastated. You may wonder why you would put any cash in a decoy wallet at all, but if someone is taking a risk by committing a crime and they get nothing, they can get upset. I don't need any upset thieves near me, so I intentionally keep a small amount of cash on me so that if it gets stolen, the thieves get something that they're happy with and I can go about my day. I've watched too many episodes of *48 Hours* to risk it—plus it's a tactic both my mom and my aunt taught me when I was old enough to walk around with a wallet.

CHILDREN TRAVELING ALONE

I've been flying alone since I was a preteen, so I wanted to briefly talk about a few options for children. Whether or not a child is ready to fly alone will be up to the parent. If you're not only a Mom Friend but also an actual mom, make sure your children are confident enough to ask for help if they need it and that they know who to ask for help. Teach them how to scream and assert themselves. Instruct them how to navigate an airport and the basics of travel.

Once you're confident your child knows the basics, there are other measures you can take. Most airlines require children who are traveling alone and between the ages of five and fourteen to travel as an unaccompanied minor. For children ages fifteen to seventeen, the service is optional. Flying as an unaccompanied minor comes with an extra fee, and it allows an adult to accompany the minor to the departure gate until the flight takes off. Once the flight is boarding, an airline attendant takes over, helping the child to their seat and with their luggage. When the flight lands at its destination, an approved adult can meet the child at the gate. If the adult is late, the airline attendant will take the child to a supervised room where they will wait until the adult arrives. Unaccompanied minors also get early boarding privileges, and if the flight has connections, there's a kids-only lounge at many larger airports. Not all airlines allow unaccompanied minors, so you'll have to call ahead to see if the service is available.

You'll also want to make sure that your child knows to wait for the attendant to escort them on and off the plane and to not wander off on their own. They should also be able to identify uniformed team members at the airport and know who to contact in case of an emergency and how to contact them.

In addition, you can use some of the safety recommendations previously mentioned. Pick flights that arrive during the day and avoid connecting flights. When you get to the gate, ask the airline who will accompany your child and whether another passenger will be seated next to them. Also, don't leave the airport until the plane takes off. Sometimes there can be an issue with the plane and the passengers might have to disembark, so stick around in case there are any unforeseen travel interruptions. Remember that food and drinks are limited on planes, so pack the essentials, including their favorite snacks—and don't forget fully charged electronic devices for entertainment.

And, of course, use technology to your advantage. If your child has a phone for calling you in case of an emergency, make sure the shared location function is enabled before you get to the airport. There's also a variety of family safety apps that you can rely on for location sharing, such as Life360.

ENJOY!

This chapter may have been focused on the risks when traveling and how to mitigate some of them, but I want to emphasize that travel is phenomenal, and if you can, I encourage you to do it as much as your budget and time allow. The memories I've made while traveling are some of the most precious ones I have. While I might avoid certain countries, cities, or activities because of safety concerns, I do believe that, with a little preparation, traveling is safe and a wonderful experience. Bon voyage!

Conclusion

While some of the facts and tips that I included here may be scary or sobering, please don't dwell on that aspect. By writing this book, I'm not encouraging you to get offline, go dark, and live like a hermit. I believe in doing the opposite of that. Get out, go on adventures, meet new people, and try new activities. Live your life to the fullest!

While you're out there in the world, let this book guide you through some of those safety and security questions that may come up, but do not let it hinder you. Remember, this book was written by a girl who has worked on national television, has traveled to more than thirty countries, has traveled alone as a minor, has skydived, and has millions of followers online—I'm not a recluse or loner. I'm a responsible extrovert who has learned from some bad experiences but has never let those dictate how I live my life.

I encourage you to live the same way! Hopefully now you'll hear my Mom Friend voice in your head as certain situations come up (#sorrynotsorry), and you'll adjust accordingly. You'll be alert and armed with a ton of go-to tips to turn to if you need them, but remember that no one can gauge a situation better than you who is living it. Trust your instincts and have confidence in yourself. You got this!

Cathy

Acknowledgments

Thank you to everyone who inspired this journey and everyone who picked up this book. To my amazing husband and best friend, Brian, whose support knows no bounds. To our little bundle of joy, who was with me while I wrote most of this book. To my *abuela*, whose love of pearls inspired the Mom Friend OOTD that's on the cover of this book. She never got to see it, but the pearls continue to remind me of her.

I want to thank my aunt, who taught me the importance of travel, education, chasing your dreams, and staying positive; my friends and family, who inspired me and supported me throughout this process, including giving me the experiences behind so many of the stories I share in this book; and the team at Simon Element, who pushed me to venture out of my comfort zone. And of course, none of this would've been possible without my social media family—the TikTokers who dubbed me the official "Mom Friend of the Group" and all those who welcomed that title as I expanded to other platforms.

Notes

Chapter 1: Mom Friend at Home

1. Aaron Chalfin, Benjamin Hansen, Jason Lerner, and Lucie Parker, "Reducing Crime through Environmental Design: Evidence from a Randomized Experiment of Street Lighting in New York City," University of Chicago Crime Lab, April 24, 2019.

2. Marty Ahrens and Ben Evarts, "Fire Loss in the United States during 2019," National Fire Protection Association, September 2020, https://www.nfpa.org//-/media/Files/News-and-Research/Fire-statistics-and-reports/US-Fire-Problem/osFireLoss.pdf.

3. "Close Before You Doze," Underwriters Laboratories, accessed September 20, 2021, https://closeyourdoor.org/.

Chapter 3: Cybersecurity: Things You Shouldn't Post and Protecting Your Data

1. "Stop Sextortion," Federal Bureau of Investigation, September 3, 2019, https://www.fbi.gov/news/stories/stop-sextortion-youth-face-risk-online-090319.

Chapter 4: Mom Friend on the Go: Safety and Convenience Away from Home

1. David Williams et al., "Assessment of the Potential for Cross Contamination of Food Products by Reusable Shopping Bags," *Food Protection Trends* 31, no. 8 (2011): 508–13; and Sarah D. Young, "Why It's Important to Clean Your Reusable Shopping Bags," Consumer Affairs, October 16, 2017, https://www .consumeraffairs.com/news/why-its-important-to-clean-your -reusable-shopping-bags-101617.html.

2. "Target Crash Population for Crash Avoidance Technologies in Passenger Vehicles," National Highway Traffic Safety Administration, March 2019, https://www.nhtsa.gov/research -data/crash-avoidance.

3. "Motor Vehicle Traffic Crashes as a Leading Cause of Death in the United States, 2016 and 2017," National Highway Traffic Safety Administration, July 2020, https://crashstats.nhtsa.dot .gov/Api/Public/ViewPublication/812927.

4. "Staged Auto Accident Fraud," National Insurance Crime Bureau, https://www.nicb.org/prevent-fraud-theft/staged-auto-accident -fraud.

Index

About the Author

Known as TikTok's Mom Friend, media personality and safety content creator **Cathy Pedrayes** sets the standard for what it means to navigate the world both on and off the internet. Cathy's first passion was environmental science, which taught her to analyze problems and seek potential solutions. She took those skills and redirected her career toward analyzing safety and cybersecurity, making resources accessible and fun one social media post at a time.

Dressed in her signature blue dress and family pearls, Cathy took to social media and gained a large following by sharing easy, everyday safety and security tips. As public interest in safety life hacks, security, travel, and cybersecurity grew, Cathy's family-friendly videos began setting viral numbers, landing her features on *Good Morning America*, Buzzfeed, *Today* Parents, and more. Her vibrant personality, innovative content, and Latinx roots have helped her cultivate a bilingual, inclusive community of people from all backgrounds aimed at making safety tips cool and accessible. Her TikTok videos alone have reached millions of views and garnered more than one hundred million likes. Cathy has also worked regularly in mainstream television; she is a former QVC host, has appeared on local news programs throughout the country, and recently began a recurring role on *The Doctors*.

As a new mom herself, Cathy intends to expand on her Mom Friend title, still in her blue dress and pearls.